Sacred in a Secular Age

Confrontations of Christian Body and Soul

AF658410

LARRY D. HARWOOD

Christian World Imprints

© Larry D. Harwood

First Published in 2020 by

Christian World Imprints
Christian Publishing & Books from India
C-3, Wazirpur Industrial Area
Delhi-110052
cwidelhi2017@gmail.com
www.ChristianWorldImprints.com
Phone: +91 11 41526079

ISBN: 978-93-5148-441-7

All rights are reserved. No part of this publication can be reproduced, distributed, performed, publicly displayed, stored in a retrieval system, made into a derivative work, transmitted or utilized in any form or by any means; electronic, mechanical, photocopying, recording or any information storage system, without the prior written permission of the copyright holder(s), as indicated, and the publishers.

Jurisdiction: Any conflict or dispute in relation to this publication shall be adjudged in accordance with the laws of India and the matter shall be subject to the jurisdiction of the Courts, Tribunals or any other Forums of New Delhi, India, only.

Disclaimer: The views, facts, contents, any copyright material used and analysis arrived at in this publication are solely of the Author(s) who assert/s the right to be identified as Author(s); the Publisher does not take any responsibility for the same in any manner whatsoever.

Printed in India.

Sacred in a Secular Age

For Mary Evangeline

"For the word of the cross is folly to those who are perishing, but to us who are being saved it is the power of God." St. Paul, I Corinthians 1: 18.

Acknowledgements

I wish to extend kind thanks to Judy Ulland of Viterbo University for a meticulous reading of the front matter in this volume and for helpful suggestions for revisions. Her willingness to help on many occasions over the past years has not gone unnoticed nor unappreciated. I also extend kind thanks to my editor, Anshul Kanda at Christian World Imprints, for her willingness to consider publishing this second collection of short stories and for her encouragement in all phases of the publishing process. Finally, and as always, I am thankful for constant and unwavering support from my wife Dottie in projects that otherwise would have been too formidable for me alone.

Preface

In 2013, I published a collection of seventeen short stories, entitled *Struggle in a Secular Age: Clashes of Christian Body and Soul*, and I was elated and grateful when my editor and publisher, Anshul Kanda, of Christian World Imprints, consented to publish a second volume of new stories in 2020. In the intervening years, I had been adding short stories alongside and for respite from other and different writing projects. I sometimes deem the construction of fictional short stories a welcome relief from the labored writings of my other main interests, history and philosophy. This is of course not to claim—because it would be palpably untrue—that fictional writing provides relief because fiction is easier to compose than the tedium involved in philosophical and historical writing.

As stated in my preface to the 2013 collection, I gravitated to fiction after witnessing the power of fiction in the layered hands of the mesmerizing storyteller. However, at times I have felt embarrassment over a tardy and childlike enthusiasm for a form of writing which most people, both inside and outside my profession and circles, appreciated long ago. Most importantly, moreover, and uppermost in my respect for fictional writing, was realization of the stunning conveyance of reality to be found in superb authors of the fictional art form. Those impressions of fiction have remained with me, indeed grown stronger, in the years between these two collections.

Finally, in this volume, like the collection published in 2013, most of the stories have religious or spiritual elements and that without apology. The age we live in (in America as well as other places) is increasingly secular, often aggressively so, and therefore I have offered in these stories some glimpses in the other direction. Shunning of the religious inclination of human nature and the denial of a religious reality as ultimately found in Christ, I believe, are profound and costly mistakes of the secular mind and spirit. Accordingly, they have been depicted as such in this collection.

Soli Deo Gloria
Larry D. Harwood
La Crosse, Wisconsin, USA
March, 2020

Contents

1

The Guest

He lay dosing, but woke himself enough to emerge from his recliner and jumped back into rumpled clothes now shoved over pajamas before heading in the direction of the door.

"I'm coming," he shouted.

A young woman stood on his bottom doorstep.

"She doesn't want to see you," he said with particular annoyance after noticing the offending book in her right hand.

Her mouth formed a smile of sorts, though she gave him no reply and in no time at all resentment for her presence escalated into a stand-off. He presumed she would spout the fanatical jargon that always offended, though she carried little of the unworldly air that usually and annoyingly displayed itself on his doorstep. Her clothes were tidy and she held herself upright with her back perfectly straight, and her black and heeled shoes evidenced polish enough to reflect the morning sun behind her. She shifted her weight just a little from one leg to the other, though otherwise she seemed prepared to stay awhile. He wondered how long the woman might stand, or how long she could withstand him.

"Doesn't want to see you I said."

The woman turned her head to look down the street, as if she might consider it time to try bothering another person at another house. She looked in the other direction momentarily, before she turned back to face him again.

"May God please go with you and then both of you'll be gone!" he said, figuring this insult to her deity might send the deity's messenger away. She said nothing and he almost closed the door on her. The past two minutes counted as more than he usually gave callers who beckoned others to their religious world. Too disgusted to resist her any longer and in probable viewing of neighbors notable for their nosiness he opened the door, figuring he might as well defeat her inside as somewhere else.

"Do you have nothing to say?" he resumed, even before he had shut the door.

"Might I have a cup of coffee?" she said, turning squarely toward him.

He scowled while a residual of constraining politeness forced him to point to a living room couch for her. After she sat he struck his head with his palm without her notice. He already regretted letting her into his house.

"Who is there?" a voice from another room had asked.

"She's asked for coffee. Come and see," he said.

A woman wearing a housecoat emerged and looked at the visitor but quickly turned her head away.

The sitting young woman held the small Bible in her right hand while crossing her arms over her chest. The house coated woman avoided the couch area and in less than a minute the sound of grinding coffee beans pervaded the kitchen. The visitor smiled to herself. The man continued to spy out his guest with a stare, but her returned look at him sent him into the kitchen where whispers began and soon adversarial voices flared between the two. When their visitor strode into the kitchen their conversation paused.

"I'm here to give you a sword, one that will give you protection and peace after it pierces your heart," she said. The two householders looked at one another quizzically. The man looked to both sides of his visitor while the young woman stared back at him.

"That some spiritual hocus pocus?" the man charged.

"We want no trouble," the woman said to the visitor, with softer words than her husband. "Neither me nor my husband want trouble," she repeated, speaking without looking at her guest and hardly loud enough to hear.

The visitor said no more as she stepped back into the living room and returned to her appointed place. Whispers resumed in the kitchen until the offended came out and now sat on the other end of the couch, though he said nothing while maintaining his scowl. In haste he stepped back to the kitchen and resumed conversation turned to argument as he picked up the phone. Perhaps someone else had the courage to do what he wanted, though he hardly had the courage to hurt his wife.

"Yes, we have an intruder," he said to his listener, while scowling at his wife.

"And you, you asked her to our house!" he whispered to his wife as he tried to explain the person of nuisance in their house over the phone.

"But you asked her in just now!" his wife said, whispering.

"So I did, but now I wish her and her sword to go!" he said, as he hung up the phone in disgust.

Two brimming cups of coffee and some tears came out of the kitchen as the woman of the house moved onto the couch beside her visitor.

"Truth is Star, I should not have asked you to come. It was my mistake, not yours. We are a conflicted family, but not all the time. If you could come another day, or better, I could meet you somewhere, just you and me. Let me know, but whatever, don't forget." The woman handed the younger woman a phone number on a scrap of paper she pulled out of her robe pocket.

"Certainly. I will be in touch," the visitor replied, as she stood up to embrace her acquaintance. The woman wanted to reciprocate the friendly gesture, though her arms stayed by her side, anxious that nothing more provoke her husband this morning.

The man emerged again, as the visitor turned to go. His hair was combed this time. "I'm going back to bed—to our bed this time. Miss, stay as long as you wish. Melissa made lots of coffee." He came over and kissed his wife's forehead and the two women soon heard the bedroom door gently shut.

"I think we can sit," Melissa said to her visitor as the two sat back down on the couch.

"He really is a good man. Most all the time tender and loving. And I do love him."

"I can see that," the young woman replied and Melissa reached to squeeze her guest's hand.

2

Jimmy Shockton's Death

Jimmy Shockton ate fava beans every Tuesday and Thursday for dinner and all other days he gobbled crowder peas, except for Sunday, when he added a salad to his meal. The green finery came tousled with bacon bits and the whole feast was drenched in runny molasses that dripped down an upturned bowl and Jimmy Shockton's large and smiling face. His parents were hardly ever amused at mealtime and almost always annoyed by anything the boy did, except for, on rare occasion, his gentler father. His mother blamed Jimmy on his father, who had divorced her six years earlier. "He never was right after you did that," she charged to Jimmy's other parent.

The man avoided his ex when he could and inched closer now to the wobbling figure of his new wife, who did not want to view the boy in death any more than she had in life. The divorced couple continued to banter blame, though Jimmy Shockton did not hear any of it. The still warm body in front of them did not move, except for a tardy joint muscle that retracted enough for one finger to visibly twitch. The miniscule but quick twitch startled Jimmy Shockton's step-mother and she jumped and then screamed to her husband that they must leave as she snatched her sweaty hand out of his. "That thing might rise up and walk on its own!" she shouted as she ran out of the house and away from the spooky life-like corpse. Her husband's eyes fastened on his son, trying hard for the moment to forget his wife and his ex as he tried desperately to remember his deceased son.

Jimmy Shockton had left as the arguments became harder to hear while painful memories dissipated into residuals that in a few more minutes vanished from Jimmy Shockton's mind. There were plenty of tables and lights that seemed none too bright for anyone else except the newcomer, so someone handed him a hat with visor to deflect some of the glare. Throngs of people walked about as pleasantries issued from each conversation that included him. Soon a pair of faces with widening smiles came closer to Jimmy Shockton and he began to feel all right in his new home as he recognized his guardians. "Angels we were and are," they confirmed to him, and they made appointment to confer later, because the meal was about to begin.

"Come to the table" a voice ahead of him spoke, and with aid Jimmy Shockton stepped forward slowly and then sat down with assistance and some pomp at a place with his name inscribed on a gold nameplate. On a nearby pedestal lay a big book, from which an attendant informed him his name had been copied. The letters were done beautifully as was befitting such a grand place and the inauguration of a new life. He paused to give thanks until the other attendant told him thanks would be received after the meal, and then Jimmy Shockton spotted the food coming and despite his best efforts, tears too. He wept but for a few seconds, for almost immediately the Host came to comfort and greet him and Jimmy Shockton moved off his chair and feel to his knees and then his new body took hold and he shook with tremors until he felt the touch that raised him up. Soon the food was served, and as he ate he wiped his mouth and his eyes.

"You neglected our boy because of that floosy," Jimmy Shockton's mother charged, turning her argument against Jimmy Shockton's step-mother, while she charged Jimmy's father with being grossly miserly toward the boy. It was true that the new wife had wanted little to do with a step-son whose medical expenses strained his father's finances and deflected her husband from due attention to her. Jimmy Shockton's father meanwhile tossed his own curses back at Jimmy's swearing mother, while Jimmy's step-mother screamed from the boiling car as Jimmy Shockton finished his first meal of fava beans while hearing none of them.

3

The Pregnancy

"I knew you had made application. For your passport I mean."

"You have followed me?" he asked, turning his head and looking at the accusing woman.

"She cares about you," she said. "She asked me to come have a word with you."

He stopped. "I already have my ticket," he said, showing her. "There is nothing I can do. You go home and let me be. I'll attend to my life and you attend to yours," he added.

"She has your child you know," she said.

"So?" he snapped.

"Is this the first one for you?" she asked.

His face tightened. This woman he had never seen until three minutes ago, when she had nudged her way next to him.

"Mind your own business!" he said, and he turned to face the front again.

"She has no one else; if no one comes alongside her, she and the baby will be alone in the next months."

"None of my concern, not now anyway."

"None of your concern?"

"I didn't force her into anything."

"She is bearing your child."

"Yea, and now she has another choice to make."

"And you've already made your choice?"

"I guess so."

"And that's that? Surely you can't be as uncaring as that?"

"I'm busy. Leave me alone."

"So you'll retreat and she'll have to fend for herself?"

"Look, mind your own business and I'll mind mine."

"You're not minding your business. That's why I'm here. I'm trying to tell you, she needs help and she feels desperate. You can't leave everything for her to manage on her own. Everything is on her without you."

"You want money? Is that what it will take to get rid of you?"

"Never mind me. This is about her and you and your child. That's your family and you need to mind it. They will not see you again if you go away and you don't care? Don't you think they want a husband and a dad around?"

"You make it sound like we're some kind of family. We're not."

"You can't be serious?"

He stared at her as his words turned to profanities, but then slowed and after a few more seconds, stopped.

"I am pleading with you. Don't walk away. Two people in the world are going to desperately need you. Don't pretend otherwise. You will hurt them deeply for the rest of their lives if you just walk away. Being out of their lives is no solution. Its cowardice and it would be irresponsible. This little one may never know you if you take off like this before the birth."

"I can't help right now."

"Now is when they need you, the mother needs you right now and will for a long time. Can't you share your life with them? Do you know where she is right now?"

He looked as if he wanted to know, but he put no words forward and Sally decided it would be best to wait him out, so she did.

He looked away and at her and then away again before he spoke.

"Where?"

"On her knees in church. She told me she felt without hope when you shrugged her off and told her you were going. She's praying right now that I might be successful in getting you to at least come and talk to her again. I don't know if I can bear to face her, I mean if I go back to her with nothing to say from you that can be of some comfort to her," she said. "I can't go back and tell her what you just told me. Tiago, the worst thing in the world for a human being is to know they are not loved by somebody who can and should love them. Don't do that to her or to your child."

"Look, I had no raising myself, no parents to speak of. How can I give to her and a baby what I never had?"

"I'm sorry your life was like that, but then don't let that happen to your child. Don't let that child be without a father, and without you around the little one will have no father. Don't let him, her, suffer like you did. You still feel the hurt of that, and what are you, thirty years old?"

"Twenty-eight. No, I don't want that for them, but she knows what she can do and she is off the hook."

"But the child will not be off the hook."

"The child has the least to lose of anybody by not coming into this beastly world."

"Beastly world? And you are making it better with the plans you have? Surely you don't mean the child is being shown a favor by being denied entry into the world! No! This child has everything to lose—a precious thing we call life. How dare you talk that way about someone who is dependent on you and a mother." Try as she might, Sally could not resist striking Tiago across the face with a hard slap. He walked away and never looked back.

"I need to get off this plane," he said.

"That is impossible Sir."

"Do what you have to do. Make it happen. You can stop this thing; you started it."

"I am afraid that is impossible and no. I'm not the pilot."

"I demand to see the pilot."

"That is not possible Sir; we are preparing for takeoff. Sit back in your seat. The pilots are fastened in and waiting for our turn to get on the runway."

"I don't need to fasten in because I'm getting off."

"Sir if you don't stay in your seat, I will have to take measures that will bring a lot of trouble for everybody and you especially."

"What is the problem?" the pilot asked.

"I must get off this plane."

"Why?"

"I have my reasons."

"They better matter more than turning around three hundred thousand pounds of steel and a packed cabin of passengers wanting to feel this plane airborne."

"A child."

"A child?"

"Yea, I fathered a child."

"So have I. I didn't have to stop any plane because of it."

"I need to see the mother."

"I need to get this machine into the air. You'll have to stay on this flight."

"Listen, I'm getting off. I'll open one of these side doors if need be."

"If you do that, your family will be visiting you in prison and not for a weekend; I suggest you stay seated and calm down before the problem escalates. The best we can do is get you on a return flight when we get to our destination."

"I can't do that."

"You'll have to, and that's a lot better than being put in cuffs and being visited in a jail cell and then in prison. Listen, if this is a real emergency we can get you on a return flight when we land. You'll be back here in a few hours."

"How few?"

The pilot looked at his clock. "Realistically, about six."

"Can I use my phone for just a couple minutes, no more, to call my family and tell them I'll be a little late?"

"Two minutes, nothing more."

4

The Book

The burly human specimens on the ground scoffed at the pathetic figure waving his weighty book from the second floor window. The gentleman covered his left ear against the maddening noise of jackhammers upending the normal etiquette of a class pondering great literature, and this day, a great poem. The book-waving professor's agitation over the disinterest of his students had surpassed his annoyance at the deafening noise below, until he dropped the book. When the unfortunate object fell workers howled with laughter that a grown man would grieve over a book. The professor now cuddled his face in his hands while the recipient worker below kicked at the doomed volume at his mercy and his feet.

For the entertainment of his audience and himself the new book owner lifted the object from a mass of broken concrete and feigned interest in the pages before he tossed the helpless book back down. With peals of encouraging laughter he threw the tip of his weighty jackhammer onto the vulnerable book, giving the object savage and brutal beating. The ramming point plunged down through a weighty text and provoked louder and coarser laughter on the ground. The ugly sound of the walloping hammer continued as the man at the window wept, his face now wet and his empty hands without his treasured book.

The project supervisor stepped away minutes before and missed the commotion, though the laughter brought him to the new owner of the mutilated book, while everyone else ceased to laugh and resumed work. The entertainer's face flushed red when confronted, and beads of perspiration poured from every effort to extract the hammer's shaft from a thousand page text. The encircling pages squeezed the hammer point, preventing easy extraction even by such a muscular worker. The supervisor counted the seconds of delayed work while the worker panicked, desperate to remove the seared book from the guilty hammer tip. When the supervisor had seen enough, he lost all patience and the worker lost his job, though the humiliated man gained a ravished book and a forgiving professor by afternoon, after the worker's supervisor insisted the worker make personal apology for his destruction. Afterward the fired worker gained a friend and the professor a listener.

"You are absurd," the teacher said to his students two days later. The words were the same words tossed at the mocking construction crew two days before. In the interim the professor had permitted the new probationary student to take up the class, though this only provided the students with more opportunity for mischief. All might have gone well if the student had better abilities, but when laughter commenced over the student's difficulty with reading words and his inordinate pronunciation, the professor tried ordering the jeering students out of the room. Only two left as the uproar persisted and Professor Smith looked on helplessly.

The gaping hole in the middle of disgraced pages stained with black dirt and yellowed grease added greater embarrassment for the new student, while the pained stares of the professor did nothing to silence students caring nothing for this professor, or great literature for that matter, nor for this latecomer, who despite their laughter, stumbled forward in the text anyway. With the obvious agitation of his professor and himself, the burly student suggested to his professor the pair ignore the commotion as the reader continued to try the written page, though hardly with any success at all. Soon unable to follow his own advice, the new student rose up and lunged at the ill-mannered and mocking students. His calculated feint hardly fooled any, as the large construction-worker-turned-student crashed into the wall behind them. The confrontation might have lasted longer but for the commanding knock at the door.

The conversation was brief and to the point. The security officer explained that complaints from portions of the campus community about the uproar from the room two days ago had brought him over. And just now he had received a call from the construction supervisor working beneath Professor Smith's classroom.

"My boss until two days ago," the new student piped up.

"Yes. He told me about the incident with you and Professor Smith and about your apology," the officer said, as he studied the student's face. "Welcome to the University," he said. The new student gave a weak smile. "But your old boss called me about this commotion in the classroom right now. Said it was so loud that he heard it despite the sounds of his men's jackhammers from below. He and I wondered if you were okay, Professor Smith."

The teacher nodded, but maintained silence while the security officer looked at him.

"I came over here Alex, because no one on this campus, except apparently some unruly students in your classroom, want to see you subjected to anything like this, not again anyway. You remember the incident we had about three years ago. The university will not tolerate that kind of thing happening to you anymore, and to show it they are prepared to act. That's why I'm here. I have two colleagues with me around the corner if we need them."

Professor Smith was silent.

"Alex, I do not want to overstep you, but a day ago I made an inquiry about the earlier disturbance and was told students can be suspended for disruptive behavior that is deemed serious enough and from what I heard in your classroom coming up just now, there is that. Anyway, the university is prepared to suspend these students for their actions."

Two pairs of eyes turned to the instructor who dropped his eyes after more moments of silence.

"How long would the suspension be?" the professor asked, his head still down. "I would not like for their schoolwork to suffer for this infraction," he continued.

"What I have here says a week," the officer responded.

"And you've got the paperwork?" the professor asked.

"Yes. Good for a week of suspension. Admin already signed off. The only signature needed now for it to be official is yours."

"But I would need to see them first, I mean before issuing this to the students?"

"No. You need only sign it. We deliver it to the students, and then we take our copy back to admin afterward. Simple as that."

"I see. And you've got the paperwork."

"Yes."

"And all that is needed is my signature?" the professor asked.

"Yes. We just bring the copies over to the admin building after serving them to the students."

"Let's do it," the new student said to Professor Smith.

"The security officer and I will do it," the teacher said to his new student, the professor's head no longer down and his words suddenly crisp. "You'll need to work on the poem. But first give the officer and me a few minutes and then you and I can go back in the classroom after the suspensions are served," the teacher said. "And I think I have another copy of the text that you can use," the professor added.

The new student dropped his eyes for a moment, though he did thank his professor.

"We will work on the poem together," the professor added.

"Certainly," said the new student.

5

The Burning

He gasped for air while his wife considered smashing her husband's dropped head with the weighty pail. She thought better and emptied it and then stepped off the back porch and ran inside the house. The dog had barked incessantly from the front yard and then scrambled around the side, though the animal remained no less excited when Morgan came out of the house holding the first towel she snatched. In near silence and standing almost motionless in a wooded lot only a hundred yards away, pigs observed the commotion at the back of the house. Morgan's husband Reginald grabbed the holey towel and swiped it across his head and then his face before he threw the near rag up onto the porch. With the flexing spigot pipe the man steadied himself as his arms shook, with breathing as violent as Morgan had ever seen, except when her husband almost drowned in a neighbor's catfish pond the past summer after drinking too much.

"Didn't know it'd be like this," he said. "Come here," he said, with his eyes finally open as he reached for her.

"I love you," he said and then Reginald shouted the same words again as Morgan's forehead felt the shaking wet cold fingers of his hand. His arm wrapped around her head and he turned to look at her and then he turned away and back again and kissed her cheek and then the other. She wished she could be impressed and so she would try. Morgan began to mutter a prayer for herself as he pulled away and his head dropped, as apology after apology came out of his mouth with words admitting the sordid deeds of a sordid life, punctuated with his pathetic plea that he was sorry. She had heard it before.

"I repented two hours ago, like your preacher said we's supposed to do, if we aint' to get our due, nor me mine—that is God's judgment," and then he sobbed for another minute before he raised his head again. His red and bulging eyes looked at her like a condemned man who pleads for mercy knowing he deserves none.

"I know you only supposed to do it once, but do it again," he said and he planted his knees firmly back into the imprinted ground. She filled the pail under the spigot again and paused again before she poured the water. The cool water dripped from his face and head and neck. Then he pulled his shirt off.

"One last time," he said, "for the Holy Spirit." Morgan almost managed to smile a little as she did pour the presumed final bucket—unless her husband had misunderstood the Trinity, she thought to herself. She regretted such mockings as soon as they came into her head and she prayed for strength to curb her sinful thoughts. Morgan's walk with the Lord suffered because of her husband she protested. He was unsteady at best and savage at worst, though she would never blame all painful things in their marriage only on Reginald.

The man on his knees and now with his forehead on the wet ground was familiar with little besides carousing and other vices like shoplifting and indecent exposure from drunkenness, and some of such behaviors on display virtually every week of their married life, until six am this morning—he said. Listening to Reginald outlining his new life while she still lay uncomfortably in bed that morning had proved unnerving. His new life began to sound like it might be as painful for her as his old life, starting with his insistence that morning to burn their house down. She had not counted on something as drastic as what he had proposed.

She would have to convince him of some other measure, though he insisted they would have to change everything for the new man he would now be in Christ. She could easier believe that he might make the new life for them so miserable that she might yearn for the old one again.

Thirty minutes after the sun came up that morning he had claimed to her to be different, though Morgan would have to have more than a few words of not only unsure repentance. More difficult was the bizarre contrition about burning the house that sounded insane. Meanwhile, against such thoughts, she would try to help him, and in so doing help herself, while she desperately tried to mute her worst thoughts. When Morgan had awakened to not find her husband beside her, though she never expected him to be at home with her every night, she remembered they had gone to bed together hours earlier. When she sat up and saw his truck keys she lay back down before she heard him and then she saw his wiry frame standing in the doorway of the bedroom. He had a blank though hardly dangerous look, one that she had scarcely seen before, or not for a long time anyway. His eyes surveyed the room and then her.

"What is it Reg?" she asked.

"Just you and me and Him from now on," he said and he looked around the bedroom as if doing inventory.

He had shown remorse in the past, but all such episodes ended on a resuming note of the old life coming back to life. His previous reformations on average never lasted beyond sundown on the same day they commenced. She wondered why she had not left him for good, just as she tried to put her own thoughts of that away for now. She would not flatter herself with any presumption of acquired sainthood for the years she had endured with a man who had most often scarcely acknowledged her. In fact, she resented herself and her sniveling posture toward him as much as she resented him, for she had tolerated a man who for years now had lived as if she did not, and she had done pitifully little, almost nothing, about it. When she had run off on two occasions, it was no better after she returned, for he mocked her failed attempt. She had had no better place to go—her parents told her she had no permanent place with them till she left Reginald for good. After a while she quit her sporadic and never successful leaving and instead just settled in, living life by herself as best she could with him around or not, sober or drunk, womanizing or not.

"We gonna have to get rid of this, maybe all of it," he had stuttered and Morgan had said nothing, fearful that she might provoke him, so she prepared for a needed escape with her back against the headboard for leverage. She mapped her route in advance, as she had had to do on previous occasions, should he come after her, though this time he staggered out of the room and she heard more commotion in the next room and then the ripping sound of objects yanked off the wall. In years previous he had taken her pictures off the wall and burned every one of them in the front yard. She did not know what he objected to with the pictures and she dared not ask for fear he might turn to further destruction. Before she had given up her efforts, she replaced a few pictures, but after a few days he took them down too and placed them under the tires of his truck and peeled off over them. He brought one back into the house, with tire smudge marks across the creased glass and hammered it back on the wall, with a nail through the center of the picture. She took it down the next day with his framing hammer, which he hardly used anymore for work. Nothing else ever went up on the walls and nothing was ever said. Her house was the only home she knew of lacking anything on the wall.

Suddenly she heard a thud outside and daring to open the curtain a little, she saw the television had been tossed out into the backyard. Soon he was back at the foot of the bed again and now she figured she would have to reason with an unreasonable person before worse came to worst.

"Everything got to go. They ain't nothing of us here, not anymore. We'll make it now. Everything else is junk—I was junk. But I ain't what I was. We got to get rid of it all. Where's my lighter?" he asked.

"Reg we can't burn this place down. We got no other place to go."

"But I got to get rid of it, every reminder of it. The old me lived here, in sin."

"Reggie you did, but we can still use this house to live in—we got to live somewhere. You never did any fornication in this house, did you?"

"No. I never did. I was a fornicator but not in our house. But I was here, I mean the old me lived here; I can't stand to live in a place that reminds me of him. We can live in the truck if we have to."

"Reggie it's not big enough. Your legs are too long for it anyway," she said, now in a near panic.

"Or I can put a cover on the back with beds and stuff back there in the bed of the truck. Or we'll live in your church. We can sleep on the pews at night and people there will help us get a new place going. They been after me for years to get my life right and now I'm gonna do it. But I got to get rid of all the junk and reminders of my sinful life if I'm gonna be a new man."

"Reg you can do that in this house. Believe me, we can make this place work. We don't have to burn it. All our things are inside it. We'd have to remove them before the burning."

"They need burning too! We's got to start over, completely over. You'll see what I did with the television when you come outside! And you'll see what I'm gonna do to that truck!"

Morgan was now in a near panic and knew she must absolutely keep him away from matches and she sprang out of bed and into action. Because she feared the thought of fire engulfing their dwelling, water sprung into her mind and the thought that she might baptize him next to the back porch, though she had no such authority from her church or from anywhere else to do so. When she offered, Reginald immediately consented and scurrying to get outside, and dropped on his knees while Morgan fetched the pail they fed their hogs kitchen scraps from. When the baptism was over Morgan felt relieved and started to feel better until he started talk about burning again,

"I got to burn that truck. I fell to so much temptation in that thing. And the godless places it took me!" His head dropped. "Yea, I got to burn it. I couldn't bear now you ridin in it with me, not anymore." He started to weep.

Morgan starred and watched while her mind went to work again.

"You promise me that you truthfully never had another woman in our house?" Morgan asked and shut her eyes. He would have to speak; a mere nod would not suffice.

"No."

"Never?" she asked.

"No, never. And I never brought any one of them women here. Not even when you wasn't here. Morgan I'll never do anything again, like my old self did, like that I mean, never again, never."

"Okay. I'll help you with the truck," she said.

"You'll help me?"

"Yea, I'll help you burn it."

"Okay."

"But we'll not burn the house."

For the first time he looked up and spoke at the same time. "Okay," he said.

They went about their duties separately and Reginald went for a can of kerosene and Morgan for matches in the house.

"Maybe you should move the truck further from the house," she said. "It's too close, it might catch I mean."

"I can't drive that truck again, not even that little bit," he said, bitterly, and their eyes met briefly.

"We can push it," she said.

"Okay."

They both pushed from the tailgate while his broad and bare shoulders rubbed against hers. For a few wondrous seconds she had, perhaps by the same unimagined grace of God that had visited her husband in the wee hours of the morning, a vivid reminder of their first and happy weeks together when they had wed a decade earlier. The recall of those earlier and wondrous times put her in the mindset of a new beginning and now she regretted every doubt about him she had allowed into her thoughts this morning. If he had been visited by God, maybe this was God's confirmation to her that what her husband had spoken would be real for them now. She shed a few tears, as happiness soon overwhelmed her as her grievances slipped away.

Reginald had been a highly skilled framing carpenter and almost never without work in their earlier married days, before alcohol and other women had started to intervene and disrupt his work first and then their marriage. Morgan had thought she could woo him back to more sober and one woman times. From the beginning her efforts hit the wall that her husband proved himself to be, instead of a bulwark of husbandly strength for the both of them.

Neither had been church goers at the time of their marriage, but as troubles escalated into serious problems and drastically diminishing happiness, Morgan started attending the church only about two miles from their house. Reginald went on occasion and was actually friendly toward the pastor there. The man gave Reginald sound advice for cleaning up his life, but the wayward Reginald acted on none of it, and his wife became discouraged and distraught when it was evident her husband would live no differently after attending church than he did without.

When she mentioned the non-difference to the pastor, he told her church-going and churches and preachers can point hearers and listeners to Christ, but her husband, like the rest of us, need Christ Himself to set us aright. "Your husband needs to encounter Christ, and be confronted by Him. Reggie needs to start with His Word. That will change Reggie into the man you are missing." Now the wild looking husband she had confronted from her bed only hours earlier seemed tamed, and she figured, tamed by Christ. A visit to her pastor was now in motion, she hoped, and maybe with

Reginald in tow, or perhaps leading. She felt immediately sorrowful for the skepticism she had felt earlier over this new husband, and especially for fear that his new life might lessen her own. Despite such regret, it was but temporary as she looked at her new husband.

The perimeter of the woods were only about thirty yards from the back porch so they pushed the truck near to the woods. Reginald spat on the truck as he walked away, and before he fetched the container of kerosene and splashed it across the truck body, though most of the flammable liquid he poured across the seats. He looked at Morgan, holding the matches, and asked for them. He reached to the ground and pulled up some dying grass and tied other dead grass around the little bundle of shriveled and dry stuff to make a ball and then he lit the object and threw it into the front seat. The flames shot to the roof of the truck cab at once and the two people stepped further back for more distance. Within five minutes the fire exploded the gasoline tank on the vehicle while the blast shook the ground beneath their feet. Both watched in silence as Morgan gazed on the scorched and blazing truck while her husband stared at the ground.

"How we get the pigs to market now?" she asked, turning to him.

"You were right that we did right doing this. I couldn't look at that truck without thoughts of what I had done in it and because of it. Getting' pigs to market is a minor worry now and I'll make sure neither the pigs or we suffer because of it. I'm going to work on giving you no more major worries. With God's help and yours, I won't be only a disappointment to you anymore. The Psalmist says to turn our eyes from worthless and sinful things—your preacher, now my preacher, says that all the time. That truck had to go. Thank you for helping me."

"Just a minute. I'll be right back," she said.

"Remember this?" she said on returning.

"Yea, the Bible you gave me. But I threw it away. That was several years ago, I think," he said.

"Well, I rescued it," she said, smiling a bit more now.

"Are you giving it back to me?"

"If you want it."

"How could I not want it?" he asked, while he held his hand out for the mutilated book. "Just one thing," he said, after he opened the initial pages.

"Yes?"

"I'll have to mark out my old name in the front here, and write over it. Because I'm a new man now," he said.

"Fine by me. We'll get a pen in the house for you," she said.

"Then let's go to the house," he said.

"Let's go to the house," she said, and she took and gripped his hand.

"I'm glad we didn't burn it," he said.

"Me too," she said, as she leaned over and kissed him.

6

The Wife

Elliot Sanders spent all but one remaining piece of change in his pockets for ice cream for the girl and Eliot knew not how to tell his wife. After a pointless trip to a bank afterward where he had no money in any account and never had, no other plan for the future was envisioned and he made contorted expressions of desperation to his companion. The girl continued to gush over the ice cream, while Eliot hoped she could offer help with his dilemma.

"She's a hard woman," he said, as he warned the girl to expect fulminating and no understanding or sympathy from his wife. Eliot actually feared for the girl's safety and tried to caution her of the risks, inexperienced as she seemed. Such advice was unneeded save for the fact that the girl had insisted on going home with Elliot. He had at first resisted, though when his anxiety of fear for her safety subsided on witnessing her courage, he gushed with praise for the youngster.

The fact of possible safety in numbers, meaning two against one, gave Eliot greater advantage with his companion than when he normally came up against his wife alone. Eliot hardly considered such as he dreamed of other and more pressing matters. "I couldn't make it in this world without you," he insisted to the youngster, his cheeks burning a little with embarrassment over words he had used with a dozen unsuspecting women in his past. He paused for a brief moment, realizing that he could still feel, and feel anew, despite a nagging wife.

The girl, not that far behind Elliot in maturity, was much further behind in years, but that scarcely mattered to Elliot who never resisted praise nor companionship from anyone who offered. His wife had ceased with any praise of anything about Eliot less than a year after their marriage. Eliot was forced to seek elsewhere for the praise essential for any human being to survive in a cold and unfeeling world.

"The woman is stone cold," he told the girl. "And to you, she will be even colder," he warned. "That's because she will resent you for seeing something in me that she's never seen," he said.

He remembered how he had told her he could endure no more of her litanies of his shortcomings, and that she would have to search for affections and praise from elsewhere.

"She gave me her blessing when I said it. Said she wondered why it had taken me so long to discover this as an option, and said she had hoped I would leave even before we had our first anniversary of tormenting marriage. Heartless, and cold I say she is," Eliot said. He needed someone who would hold him up, not always pull him down. He had wanted a new life for some time and this girl seemed the latest bit of aid in a needed step forward.

He had spotted the girl walking his direction on his way toward one of his fishing spots only hours earlier.

"Not gonna catch much fish without a pole of some sort," he had said to the girl as his first words to this stranger, with scarcely any idea whether the girl had any intention of fishing or not. She didn't say anything right away, but she did continue in his direction, though looking Elliot over to the point that her stare caused him after about fifteen seconds to throw his eyes to the ground before he threw his body on the ground to fake one of his seizures. The seizures did not always happen when he needed them and he needed one right then, because Eliot could see potential for himself in this damsel. He had no evidence for any intelligent estimation of this stranger, for the girl did nothing but observe the body in contortions and after two minutes of throwing his arms and legs about and scraping up and accumulating a pile of dirt from his shoe heels plowing the ground sideways, he stopped to permit a secretive glance at her, for he always closed his eyes at first when he faked a seizure. The girl stood without any motion and he started to think the contortions were perhaps too traumatizing for a person of her young age, and so he dissipated his jerking motions entirely and began to groan instead. Finally she closed the distance of ten or so feet that she had maintained from his previously gyrating body and even asked him if she could help. After the girl aided his getting up and then walking upright, he had offered to take her to the soda shop.

Over the small cups of ice cream that Eliot could afford, the two got to know one another a little and Eliot's appreciation for the girl's kindness soon vaulted into gratifying affection from him to her. "Love does not wait for the lazy," was a proverb that Eliot had coined for use for himself and he used it often. Once he let his proverb slip out inadvertently in the presence of his wife and she said that had been her problem in first taking up with Eliot. She had mistakenly thought he was so handsome that another girl would take him if she didn't first and so she went for the gold quickly, she told him later. "I was young and stupid," she had said. "And now I have the rest of my life to pay for it, with no hope in sight of a heart attack or a stroke that could relieve me of this wretch of a husband." Eliot shook his head as he recounted her hurtful words.

After the ice creams were finished Eliot explained his love for the youngster in terms that an eighteen year could understand, despite the fact that she insisted she was nineteen and pulled out a car license to prove her birthday. Eliot was impressed even more with this documentation and slowly forgot about his explanation of love for the girl.

"You have a car, do you?" he asked.

"Yes," had been her reply. When Eliot inquired why she had been walking when she had a car, which he said made no sense to him, she had laughed, but not offensively so and so Eliot was not offended. After that she offered to take him to see her car, only about six blocks from the soda shop, and

Eliot made a game out of trying to guess which car was her car as they walked down streets with occasional cars parked on both sides. She insisted on driving after Eliot offered but also told her he had no license.

"My wife refused to give me the money for the license fee at the DMV," he complained. "I still haven't recovered from her stinginess with our money," he lamented. While the girl drove, Eliot provided final warnings of the firestorm they were certain to encounter on arriving at his house.

"It'll be really tough," he warned her again as he knocked on the door of his house and jumped back a little and waited. The girl was not forced forward of Eliot, as she herself insisted on standing in front. Of course any observer would have inferred that his position advertised his fear of the person inside. The door came open suddenly—Eliot jumped—and all the advice and warnings Eliot had provided the young girl with took a back seat to the reality both now faced.

"I told you about bringing women home, young ones or old ones or any ones, without letting me know beforehand," she said. Eliot ignored the lecture "for he had all of them memorized already."

"Jen, this is Sophia, a young lady I just met. Show her some politeness or we'll be staying an even shorter time than I had planned." Eliot felt a morsel of pride for his defiant tone and he looked at Sophia for more justification for his good fortune to find her.

"Eliot have a seat here; Sophia come with me," Jen directed, and Sophia followed her. Not to be manhandled by the overbearing wife Eliot had described, Sophia jumped to his defense when she reached the kitchen.

"You know your husband's pitiful," the girl said, figuring it was best to take charge of the conversation at the beginning—one last thing that Eliot had told her on the drive over.

"And lazy," the wife responded. "And a pretender, or liar, whichever you prefer, because he's both," she continued.

"I don't understand," the girl said.

"I'm not his wife. I'm his sister," she explained.

"But he said you were his wife—"

"He pretends to be married sometimes. Makes him feel equal to other people that are married he says. He has invented a whole story of an awful wife that he tosses at people all the time, probably at you too. If he could hold a writing instrument long enough, he might write up this fabricated story and sell it for a fortune."

"But pretending to be married when he isn't?"

"Makes him seem at least a little normal," his sister said. "You see, if he's got a wife, he's done something, accomplished something. I mean then he's a man of the world, so to speak, in his eyes anyway. At least one person, once upon a time, found him congenial enough to marry—so his fabricated story goes. That's the impression he can convey if he's married, however awful the marriage might be at the moment."

"You know he told me how awful you been to him," the girl said, intent to stand her ground for a little while longer.

"You believe everything you hear?" Jen asked, mildly scolding the youngster, who decided now that she must show she was not a complete dupe.

"I kinda figured he wasn't married. I mean no ring, first thing, though I know that's not much to go on. He was so odd though I maybe got too curious. The way he shook on the ground told me he didn't really know what a seizure was. But it was his cry of help and I couldn't just ignore that. No humane person could ignore that. He did try to kiss me later for my help, I think he thought it was some kind of reward I had earned, but I told him it was too soon, I mean for anything like that. Plus, I had my spray handy if he went for broke, so I wasn't too afraid of him. I did find him curious almost beyond belief."

"Curious enough to come home with him?" Jen asked, still not sure the girl was as savvy or prescient as she implied.

"And why are you here?" the young girl asked, deciding to throw the question back on the questioner.

"Nobody else will have him. This is my house anyway. He only lives here by my good graces, and despite what he may have told you, I do not resent him. Annoyed by him most of the time, yes. He contributes very little to the expenses around here, though he does bring home a mess of fish once in a while for me to clean and cook. And he will do it most anytime I ask him. He's like a kid fishing, I mean the surprise and enjoyment of catching one! If his blood and mine weren't related, however, I'd sent him packing long time ago. But if I pushed him out or he left, he'd have nowhere to go. Family is important, even when they's unfit for about everything and anybody in this world. Plus, as I said, he brings home fish enough in the summer time to help our table and in the winter he keeps us warm enough in here with wood he cuts and chops in our woods for the heater. So

I can put up with him, most times. When I can't, I send him out. That's why he's mostly out of the house. Reckon that's how he ran into you."

The girl got up from the hard chair and walked over to the only kitchen window and looked out.

"Has he ever had a girlfriend and I'm not planning on being one. Just asking," Sophia said.

"Yea, but they almost never last long, not more than a few hours anyway. That's because it doesn't take much time spent with him to figure him out and when women do, they skedaddle. But truth be told, I'd rather he not even marry. He could never hold up the obligations in a marriage, so the marriage would be doomed from the start and the ending of it would overwhelm him, probably do him in."

"I feel a little better now. Not thinking anymore about running out the back of your place here as I was at first," Sophia said and Jen smiled a little.

"Hope you'll stay for dinner with us. We're eating a batch of bluegills Elliot caught yesterday."

"She'll be staying for dinner," Elliot shouted to Jen from the front room and over the loud television.

"As you wish," his sister said, beginning to set the table for three.

"But what about you," the young girl asked.

"What about me?"

"You've made a home for him here. How about your life?"

"My husband got killed in the war. Eliot started coming over here after that to keep me company, mainly at nighttime but pretty soon most all the time and our parents didn't mind and certainly didn't mind having him out of their house, though he wasn't as bad in those days. I knew he came over in the beginning because he cared about me, but it did take some caring after him as time went on."

"What if you happen on someone—I mean a mate?"

"Young lady, you must have lied to my brother about your age. You're too young for such questions!"

Sophia laughed.

"I do go out on occasion, but there seem no suitables for me, or none that I've found that can compete with the man I once loved and visit every week in the town cemetery. Even if I find another as good as him, I won't forget about Eliot. But it hasn't come to that yet. That's maybe the way it should stay."

Sophia was offered a small but cushy chair in the cramped living room, but declined so as to sit on the couch with Elliot. Presently, she insisted on going to the grocery for a container of ice cream as her contribution to the meal. Eliot insisted on going with her, but his sister insisted he stay while Sophia go.

"The woman is impossible at times," he said in whispers to Sophia afterward. "Sometimes I regret I married her, but then if I hadn't, she'd be ruining someone else's marriage, so I'm kind of a martyr."

7

The Examined Life

The scientific world, or nearly anyone who claimed to be anybody in it, had come to the funeral, in addition to many and notable others. Most mourners of course had not met the deceased, indeed very few people, even many of the locals had not, though everyone far and wide had heard about the man. Many stood in the elongated line at the wake, craning their neck for a look at the welded casket cradling the body that had lasted for two hundred and thirty six years until death six days earlier.

Controversy was fomenting in the wake of his death: the controversy was referred to ironically as "untimely," by some of the press.

"All that prodding from curious parties. The poor man could hardly endure and indeed it would have killed even a younger man," one charged.

He had lived for almost a year after two probing local men discovered him.

The whole episode started with inquiry to the police motivated by mere curiosity. A neighbor of the old gentleman, and new to the community, stopped into the police station one evening and made simple inquiry. There was no lodging of any complaint about the gentleman infracting the law, no disturbing the peace, nothing of the sort. The newcomer in the community found himself simply curious about his elderly neighbor after the children of the newcomer had an encounter with the old gentleman.

"Why don't you go to him with your questions?" the officer behind the desk replied, after his visitor evidenced keen puzzlement and interest in the old man.

"Well, I do know his name. John Hastings it is, but I have been hesitant to disturb him and interrupt his privacy," the inquirer said, and then followed a bit of a rambling story about how his own three children had happened on the man one afternoon in front of the old gentleman's cabin.

"He told my kids all sorts of stories."

"So?" The two officers sat and listened, but remained unconvinced that anything was unusual about the elderly man. The inquirer persisted.

"Mr. Hastings told my kids about his father's land grant and said his father got it for his service in the American Revolutionary War."

Both police officers sat up, though only a little. "John Hastings told them that?"

"He did."

"The man is old. Probably forgetful, senile. Childish, you know," they said. The inquirer would not be deflected.

"Did he have a wife, children?" he persisted.

The pair looked at one another.

"Can't say we recall anything like that. Long as we can remember, the old man has been alone."

"You never saw a wife?"

"No, we presumed if there was one, she passed some time ago. But maybe he's been a bachelor all his life."

"How about any kids he and a wife might have had?" the inquirer asked.

"They could have moved away; lots of kids do that these days. But we've never seen any visitors there either, now that you mention it. At holiday time I don't recall ever seeing any cars or guests at his cabin."

"You never saw any family come around him at Christmas time, Thanksgiving, Easter, July Fourth?"

"Well, we don't see everything."

"Does he have any relations at all in the community?"

"Can't say about that," the two said in near unison.

At first the village public records official hardly proved any more helpful when the curious neighbor continued his query there. When asked about a birth certificate on file for John Hastings, and when none was discovered, the official showed more interest.

"About what time or decade would he have been born?" the official asked. The inquirer could not muster courage enough to say something sounding so ridiculous as a man with a life more than two centuries old, and so he diverted from his inquiry enough to avoid the appearance of lunacy. After a few more minutes of small talk the inquirer quickly and quietly thanked the records official before leaving. The matter might have ended there, except for the fact that later that evening the official, Randall Potgrove, recalled the name of his inquirer as James Strudlow and found Strudlow's number in the phone book. Potgrove proceeded to tell Strudlow about some curious records he had come upon after Strudlow had left and was insistent that the two men meet the following morning at the public records office. Strudlow hardly slept that night and called in sick at his job the next morning. He spent two hours at the public records office with the official before they broke for lunch and then the two spent another hour talking in the car before they separated. Neither man had any idea yet of how closely they would be working together in coming days and weeks, nor how quickly their own lives would suffer along with Mr. Hastings.

The next day they met for lunch again and made a plan to visit the old man after work the following day.

When they arrived around seven, there was some trouble getting him to the door, though finally he appeared and summoned his visitors inside. He sat in a rocker that looked older than him.

"My grandfather's," he said to his visitors, who were motioned to some straight chairs in a room with a pot-bellied stove that took at least a quarter of the space of the small room.

"What can I do for you fellers?" the host asked his visitors, who soon had trouble deciding who would start.

"Just a neighborly visit? I see. No harm in that. I don't have many visitors, not anymore," the man said. These visitors smiled at one another, until Strudlow managed to initiate conversation, while their host eased back into the antique rocker.

"My children told me about some of your family stories that you entertained them with some days ago," Strudlow said to their host.

"Interesting that you have interest. I told them youngins quite a bit as I recall, I mean because it was quite a bit. I probably wouldn't have talked to them as much as I did if I had visitors more frequently, but I am glad you're here. Those kids probably got more than they bargained for from an old man." The old man coughed a little after he finished his words.

The two visitors looked at one other as Potgrove got out a notebook. The old man looked on curiously.

"Don't mind if I take down a few things as we talk do you?" Potgrove asked, noticing the old man's stare. The old man shook his head that it was okay.

For almost two hours the elderly man catalogued a life that was well beyond any years of usual life span. Oddly, almost as if he didn't realize it, was the old man's impression that there were surely people in the community as elderly as him. Most of the old man's tone was serious for his life had been marred by some tragedies he said, like two first cousins killed in the American Civil War, though he also told riveting stores of how he had overcome some of the strains and obstacles of what sounded like at least three usual lifespans. When the cuckoo clock sounded at nine o'clock the old man looked visibly fatigued and his voice diminished as his visitors insisted that they must be going and stood up. The old man told them to come again in a few days after he had rested up. "That was just a smidgen of stuff I told you tonight," he said. "Plenty more where that came from," he continued. The men smiled.

The next evening the two interested men met at Potgrove's house, in his basement. He had made copies of pertinent documents discovered in his office that day and the day previous and had also managed to date within the spread of a few years, some of the stories the old man had told the two men at their visit. The documents and the graph of a timeline were spread over two sheets of plywood pitched on four sawhorses he had bought at the hardware store. Strudlow did not leave until midnight and both men agreed to also meet the following evening, though this time at Strudlow's residence.

The next evening the two men verified as best they could everything from the prior evening, with Potgrove suppling two more documents to add to their knowledge of the life of Mr. Hastings, one of which was the first federal census taken in America in 1790, with a Mr. Hastings listed as a head of household. By the end of the evening, the two men concluded that Mr. Hastings seemed as ancient as Strudlow had initially been led to believe, though Potgrove admitted to Strudlow he had given assent twenty four hours earlier, but had had to satisfy his combative skeptical inner nature before he could openly agree. Moreover, because such surmise about the longevity of Mr. Hastings seemed more the stuff of fantasy than fact, the men spent much of the evening conferring on the seeming impossibility of what they believed they had found. They admitted the possibility that further scrutiny of the collected documents might in fact divulge the existence of more than one man, collapsing their surmise of one man with over two centuries of life behind him. The possibility of something other than that, however, seemed hardly plausible, for it suggested gross deceit or manipulation or record keeping incompetence or perhaps a suspicious conspiracy of some unfathomable motivation. Mr. Hastings himself seemed quite incapable of such a complicated endeavor, and Potgrove in coming days revisited the logs of visitation at the public records office for anyone that might have conducted prior research on Mr. Hastings, though he found nothing there suspicious. Both Potgrove and Strudlow nevertheless at times wished something would turn up that could account for or resolve the conundrum of a man appearing to have lived a life way beyond a normal life span, for their efforts would soon so strain the two inquirers that their own lives began to unravel before that of the elderly Mr. Hastings.

Though the two men had made a pledge to one another for absolute secrecy over the matter, in only a couple days, rumor emerged of Potgrove and Strudlow's discovery of Mr. Hastings's alleged but unbelievable longevity. How the guarded secret leaked out in a mere matter of hours was unknown to either Potgrove or Strudlow, with each assuring the other that he had maintained strict confidentiality. Moreover, community suspicions about the two men soon escalated, particularly as they were seen frequently at Mr. Hastings's cabin. Adding fuel to the fire of incessant talk was every idiot's undisciplined speculation about how a man could live to such an unheard number of years. Partly to bring clarity rather than unwarranted guesses to the mounting allegations, almost immediately the scientific community became insistent for opportunity to physically examine Mr. Hastings. Such investigators as these would be sure to diffuse the whole ridiculous matter, they contended, and the sooner the better, unless the village desired to be a laughing stock for the rest of the county. When no such permission was given by Mr. Hastings, one requester began to impugn the credentials of Potgrove and Strudlow, charging that only one of them had some training in the craft of historical analysis and that neither of the two men was a scientist.

Potgrove nor Strudlow had significant financial means. To strain such matters more, Strudlow took an unpaid leave of absence from his job as an engineer in the first week of the unfolding story. Financial resources first began to dwindle with the costs of hiring protection for privacy for Mr. Hastings, for it was necessary to keep ner-do-wells away. With small though incessant mobs and idle onlookers continuing to come, a police surveillance was requested by the two men and granted around the property of Mr. Hastings. When even this measure proved insufficient to protect the old man, Potgrove and Strudlow moved into his tiny cabin with him to exert more effort to maintain some normalcy for the old man. However, soon the energies of the two men diminished in the face of frenzied activity and Potgrove died one month later from a second heart attack on the same day as the first. An unmarried man with no relatives that he apparently thought well of enough to include as designees in his estate distributions, in his will Potgrove gave his modest savings to his friend Strudlow and Tina, Strudlow's wife, who were asked, though not required in the wording of the will, to aid in the care and keeping of Mr. Hastings for as long as they could.

Tina Strudlow had favored her husband's interest, care, and concern for the old man, but convinced her husband, for the sake of his own perceptibly diminishing energies, to come back to their home and he did. The Strudlow children, who by now were witnessing the strains of their parents and that of Mr. Hastings, were astoundingly supportive of their father and indeed both parents in their efforts for Mr. Hastings. After their father returned home, the three children managed to assist in maintaining more lookouts for trespassers. Police barricade officers devised an interface between themselves and the three youngsters for their common purpose of protecting an old man whose life was close to an undeserved end by being brought to the notice of the world.

From his house and for a short while, Strudlow was able to maintain his work in the interest of the old man. In addition to Strudlow's own constant and meticulous sifting of the life story of Mr. Hastings, all inquirers and any visitors for the old man had to come through Strudlow. As taxing as visitors were upon the old man, the hordes of hopeful visitors were more overwhelming for Strudlow and he suffered a debilitating stroke less than another month after Potgrove's passing. At this point Strudlow's wife Tina took charge of most of what her husband had been doing in addition to maintaining full responsibility for a household and now care for a frail husband. Not one to grumble or dither, Tina Strudlow approached a sitting agency for voluntary aid to care for the old man in his cabin. The work of these laborers provided her time enough to maintain some modicum of civilization in her own household and the conveyance of some due respect for a man who was over two centuries old.

Mrs. Strudlow required each person desiring an appointment with the old man to construct a thousand word application justifying the need for appointment. After her husband's stroke, she permitted, all total, only sixteen visitors with fifteen minutes of visitation time each before the day of Mr. Hastings's death. Two of the sixteen, visitors 3 and 14, were found to have collected unauthorized specimens for DNA analysis from the old man's saliva, without any prior request to do so from her or Mr. Hastings. The two men were each charged with a misdemeanor for their misdeed and put to trial and convicted. The two DNA specimens remained unaccounted for. Meanwhile, Tina, with Mr. Hasting's permission, moved him in with the Strudlow family and took steps to have his humble cabin boarded up. Mr. Hastings never slept another night in his own bed or cabin.

Meanwhile, James Strudlow began to improve a bit from his stroke, and with help from his children, he returned for brief periods of work to the notebooks he had kept concerning Mr. Hastings when he and Potgrove had first discovered the aged man. Also included were three half hour interviews that Strudlow had with the man after the death of Potgrove.

With her work of managing most everything concerning Mr. Hastings's well-being, Tina became increasingly incensed by continuing requests for DNA sample from the man, in light of the two earlier incidents. She was almost persuaded by her husband to allow the taking of a sample, subject to Mr. Hasting's consent, until she read in the required application of such a requester his boast to be able to put to an end the whole silly notion of a human being living 233 years with a sample. Such incidents were but the beginning of Tina's forays into the public sphere, where she took on, usually in newspaper opinion pieces, a defense of Potgrove and her husband's contentions about Mr. Hastings.

As if this were not enough to occupy the woman, Mrs. Strudlow soon encountered a new kind of demand concerning Mr. Hastings. On a banner hanging in the village an inscriber had demanded that the authorities be allowed to take a DNA sample from Mr. Hastings, for it was unjust, the writing said, that only one man have the benefit of these added years to eat, drink, and be merry for longer than the rest of us. In her pieces in the paper, she now criticized obsession with extending the mere years or length of life, with little consideration for the purpose of life. "Mr. Hastings," she said, "had maintained both in fine form." The worst insult to Mr. Hastings, however, was yet to come, and when news of it came to his ears, the gentleman would be dead within twelve hours.

A policeman who had been presumed to favor securing Mr. Hasting's privacy allowed a government official to come to Strudlow's wife Tina with a petition asking that Mr. Hastings be taken in as a ward of the state. The official, moreover, had insisted that this move would be in the best interest of Mr. Hastings. When Tina Strudlow began to object, the official produced another and stronger reason, he said, for taking Mr. Hastings, but a reason more repulsive to Mrs. Strudlow. This official contended that the government, due to its interests in human longevity must be cognizant of all of its human subjects and citizens and not merely one to whom the government extends unfair privilege. If it is believed that Mr. Hastings is the ripe old age so claimed, the government is preparing to assert and demand the right of the state to take his person, that is, to claim him under the right of eminent domain, as a property of the state. As such, the favor shown to his body by nature will be extended to other and all bodies and thus all will benefit. Therefore, the state asserts its rightful prerogative to declare they are taking possession of Mr. Hastings, just as any municipality can claim eminent domain for a piece of needed real estate. As compensation for the government taking Mr. Hastings under the right of eminent domain, his village and county would receive three million dollars, that amount deemed just compensation to study a man of Mr. Hastings's longevity. On hearing this pronouncement, Tina Strudlow ordered the official off her property.

The death of Mr. Hastings hardly permitted his corpse more peace than the man had in the last year of life. So determined were some hopeful viewers for a photograph of the aged corpse, that the casket was not open and the lid welded shut and security officers posted at each end. Since

Mr. Hastings had no living family known to anyone, some of the attending policemen served as pallbearers. As honorary pallbearer, James Strudlow, though in a wheelchair, was marshalled. Though Strudlow had been requested by Mr. Hastings to speak, he was foreseeably unable to do so, though he tried anyway. When a stream of tears and mostly unintelligible words issued from him his wife Tina took over, speaking from a piece of paper Strudlow had inscribed for her. The service was conducted by Mr. Hastings's pastor, a Rev. Wineska. Mr. Hastings had selected scriptural passages beforehand, and asked to read them were the three children of James and Tina Strudlow. Mr. Strudlow had requested that one of the hymns sung for his funeral be "I Need Thee Every Hour." In the only bit of humor evident in the entire afternoon, Rev. Wineska had remarked, concerning the aforementioned hymn, that God would be glad to welcome someone home whose prayers had been attended to by Him for over two hundred years. "Not only will Mr. Hastings be resting," the Rev. said.

8

The Martyr

"Will he never shut up?"

"When he feels the life draining out of him he will. Then he'll figure that god of his is no help to him."

Both of the guards laughed even as they disdained to tolerate the despicable specimen. "His misery is nothing compared to ours," one of them shouted to onlookers and a few laughed.

"I get to die for Him," their prisoner shouted, though not as loudly as he had only a half hour earlier. "My whole life I lived like a coward. Thank you Lord for your mercy," and the whip from one of his guards cracked around his torso as the blood spilled again from the gashes.

"Thank you Lord," he shouted again.

"Better cut a little deeper into him. His words will dry up then."

"Good idea," the other guard said, as he drew the whip tighter and across the prisoner's abdomen and around the back side. Blood spurted from front and back.

"Good one!" the other guard shouted and the two smiled at one another. The exasperation of the guards was set against the crowd, who preferred the whole event of taking a prisoner to his execution not come to an end. Most of the mobile crowd rather enjoyed the spectacle and a dead body was unwelcome where there had been a living one to torment while they watched.

The prisoner could hardly hear the crowd chatter anymore, or the guards for that matter, for the guards had earlier burst his eardrums by boxing his ears without mercy. They were to walk him and then finally to drag him to his execution on the hill. "Praise God!" he had said to himself no fewer than a hundred times already, though probably none of his utterances were heard as his strength for words neared depletion. He had been denied water as his walk began, three hours earlier and two miles away.

The man convicted of treason and now paying for his crime with his life had been a favored because obedient citizen of the State for three decades before admitting and then repudiating his former cowardice. Having once dutifully bowed to political pressures he now felt it incumbent he suffer for his past, and when the State had insisted that his preaching proclamations refrain from any reference to God or the Bible or Jesus anymore, he demurred. References to Christ would now be permitted only as justifications for secular principles capable of divesting themselves of anything religious and specifically Christian. Thus, for example, any allusion to Christ as the Bread of Life must be amended to be read and understood as the need for bread and not the need for Christ, but for socialism. For this previous and allegiant minister of the State, such nullifying of the Christian message was at last too much, and it could not be tolerated by him he said, not anymore at least. To the chagrin of State authorities, the man became uncooperative and finally obnoxious toward his previous masters.

The rejection of his past obedience to the State had jolted the man from one world to another and from his old life to a new one, though the man was now almost seventy years of age. Now referring to himself as "born-again," a phrase found in the Christian Gospel, he spent well-nigh a month in literal sackcloth and dusty ashes to show sincere repentance. The repudiation of his prior allegiance to a State that he now disavowed was too much for the authorities. His work and allegiance now, he said, was for Christ and His Church.

He had read his composed repudiation of what he had formerly assented to as a minister of the State on the occasion of his last sermon from a State pulpit. His "proclamation" was rewarded by the State with a public defrocking of his credentials to be a State minister any longer. Now barred from his pulpit, he promptly took up another elsewhere, in one of the so-called house churches, though in the beginning of this ploy he naively thought himself rather out of danger. Safety was presumed because secrecy was maintained, or so he and others thought, though soon virtually everything about the man's whereabouts and activities was known to the authorities. Though soon aware of danger to himself the defrocked minister nevertheless continued to preach his unauthorized message, even after his small and rural congregation, fearing for themselves, became smaller.

Beginning attempts by the State to muzzle the man were met with obstinacy on his part and infuriated the State authorities who now saw in him an utter lack of any respect for them or the State that stood behind them. Furthermore, not a single investigator of the culprit's case could possibly miss his glaring refusal to assent to any of the restrictions placed on his preaching. Soon it was decided by the authorities that something commensurate on their part with his odious civil disobedience was required and the authorities set into motion a most significant charge against him of treason. Some lesser though still very important violations were additionally alleged against him, such as not genuflecting before any officials of the State encountered in passing on the street and his refusal to take any oath required by the State that lacked a reference to his God. The belligerence of the man now became maddening to officials who were overwrought with a man who seemed to act with so little thought or care for his life. Vowing to silence him, at first short of execution and death, they hatched what seemed at first like a thoroughly reasonable plan. He was given a perfunctory trial, speedily conducted, with dubious witnesses alleging multiple instances of his criminal activity and inventing others. In an unexpected turn of event, however, the verdict and the sentence came too quickly and a watchful public clamored in protest. Their protest, however, was largely absent of any actual sympathy for the fate of the accused. Their point of interest in the man was rather that onlookers had enjoyed his display of belligerence. Amongst a population who had come to believe, because they had been repeatedly told to believe, that obedience to the State was the highest form of virtue of a citizen in society, the spectacle of his obstinacy against the State drew significant attention.

The mockery the accused subjected his accusers to provided theatre and the viewing public did not wish to see it end, for the man proved, if nothing else, that the some business of the state could also provide amusing entertainment. Meanwhile, only a few understood his actions and speeches by way of motivations on his part. To his audience and to the angered officials, he seemed bafflingly welcoming of his fate. The gratified audience saw a game of cat and mouse made pleasurable pastime because the mouse in this case did not seem to mind—indeed—seemed to enjoy defying the cat that would in time kill him. The crowd, however, resented the fact that the State would win or manipulate its way to winning against this man. Most everyone knew the accused would eventually have to fold and then their amusement would end with him ending.

The condemned man, having lost all strength to stand erect and walk toward his place of execution, now instead crawled on his bloodied flesh, in miniscule fashion, closed the remaining distance between him and a cross that lay scarcely a dozen yards away. When he could not pull himself forward anymore his two guards took turns kicking him forward, aiming their steel-toed boots in the center of the skimpy cloth that covered his extruding hips. The sharp and violent kicks managed to persuade the body a few inches forward until the annoyed guards placed a rope around the bloodied neck and the two now jerked and drug him to the cross with no assistance from him. His head finally butted the wood and he groaned but managed to turn his head enough to kiss the cross, bloodied by a prior execution. The two guards spat on the man for his abhorrent piety and snatched the body upright and then dropped it down onto the flat cross. They smiled with the collision of the back of a head against the unforgiving wood. The body convulsed while the trembling right hand of the dying man reached out to form the shape of a cross in the air. As the man's soul slipped away the drooping hand hastened to draw a second and then a third one while the men who had killed his body watched.

9

The Supplicant

The sage walked into the room for the evening class that nearly every enrolled student save one loathed. She negotiated her way to her preferred seat in front, while her classmates chatted amongst themselves in cliques of twos and threes on nothing of significant consequence, except low grades and after class parties. Two of them nodded in her direction after the green-eyed female settled into her seat. Talk among the group of about twenty hardly serious students sounded more like alley or street language of the untutored than aspiring scholars. One member of the class who almost never engaged with classmates began making gestures eliciting some laughter at his gross imitation of the mannerisms of the group's teacher. Some of the group noticed his skill and suddenly, nudged to continue, he slowly succumbed to requests and garnered their approval.

Before and in a previous class session, the mimic had impotently tried denying his skill in such spoofing, though more urgent insistence from an aroused audience this evening convinced him otherwise, and he discovered, as if by sudden revelation, that he possessed skills that until the present were untapped. For the next few minutes his audience succeeded in freeing him from his imprisoned self. The realization of what he was capable pushed the dormant youngster into awareness that he could be one of them, though his desire was not actually for any of them, except for the girl the group called the sage. He had no idea how she earned such a name, though he had managed to find out that Susan Winerod was her real name. He had imagined on occasion that she and he might be the only students deriving benefit from the class and their teacher.

Tonight, however, his envious weakness to be part of the group had overwhelmed and temporarily shredded respect for his teacher. The professor for the class was most of the time on time, and in the last minute or two before his anticipated arrival, with the nervous mimic at work before his laudatory audience, the dutiful sage got out her highlighted and well-worn text and an ample notebook for class notes. While she found her page in the text, the mimic looked her way for a positive sign of her interest as he continued to unearth more of his unmined talent. After his third impression of their teacher, he sat back in his seat, slightly exhausted by his actions though suddenly more repulsed than exhausted. Sitting silently was his usual preference during class, at least most of the time, and he slumped down a bit at his desk now, contorted like a bear preparing for a lengthy and quiet hibernation. For the moment he lost any hope of his for her notice until the sage looked backwards at him and smiled without strain. He tried to reciprocate, though he lacked the sage's easy manner. He had never even spoken to her and was not sure he even could.

The mimic had noticed the girl early on in the term, but now feared his exhibition this evening, which she could have hardly missed, had put her off. He now regretted his earlier antics and the obvious pleasure he had enjoyed as the group's entertainer, if only for a few minutes. Most everything that he ever did or tried to do on such occasions turned into crushing defeat or humiliating embarrassment. The impression he had given the sage of himself this evening was now palpably sickening to him and he considered going home when his stomach too insisted on attention. He was nearly out of his seat and headed to the restroom when suddenly his stomach settled and he returned to sit again.

The always late three or four students sauntered into the room and flopped into their seats at the back, where he usually sat too, but without really conversing with any of them, or hardly ever. He was feeling embarrassed and ashamed of himself now for his earlier performance and feared he had ruined any chances with the sage. His agony did not persist, for with the teacher still not present, she got out of her seat and walked toward him. The bawdy and loud laughter prevented anyone from hearing when she invited him out for coffee. As soon as she returned to her desk the teacher walked in and the ivory-tower talking head lectured without interruption or a student question for fifty weighty though unmesmerizing minutes for anxious students. The mimic felt only his grief pummeling him and no ability this evening to ingest any of the prof's words. The sage had her own thoughts, though these the supplicant could not grasp until later.

"I'm not like them," he said, and she smiled, again. From his lips to her ears he had divulged a mass of redundant explanation as he hopelessly tried to convey how he was not one of them. His multiple and laborious tries provoked her suggestion the two take a walk after their coffee, though the seven previous minutes of clumsy chatter almost provoked a refusal before his mind stopped his tongue and started his feet. And then she reached out for his hand. His heart did not flutter, not immediately, though his eyes went dim and he stopped walking for a few seconds as he took her offered hand. He had held other girl's hands. He dared not appear presumptuous or beggarly and he who was without hope in the next instant dropped her hand. "You are wasting your time with me," he started, though she shook her head, in a polite gesture of disagreement.

He starred at the ground as his facial muscles strained more and then his despairing face dropped lower as she took his hand again. She insisted that they still walk, though his hand became ever clammier in hers. She listened as he tried to stop undesired tears pushing outward after his words. Twice he shook his head, and she stopped walking and starred at him. "We can go on," he said eventually, and they resumed the walk as his hand grasped her hand and once she even crossed his path to switch hands. He suspected he had held her hand too tightly. A demeanor of inviting happiness hardly left her face and eventually his heart relaxed after they stood still for some time while he simply listened.

"Ever kiss a girl before?"

"None like you," he said, his face expressionless.

"It's not that complicated, not like that philosophy stuff, in fact it is quite without much effort, since the urge and movement of kissing someone you want to feel close to is virtually irresistible; I mean when someone really wants to kiss another person—I mean romantically—there is hardly any stopping them. That thought pervades the recipient while they are being kissed, and so travels along with the kiss received. And as example, it occurs right now when you find it impossible to resist kissing me and knowing that just adds to the experience, both yours and mine."

"I see."

When he tried to talk again she held up her finger.

"What?" he asked.

"Intimate things are better without words or talking, if you can manage."

"I see."

Afterward she told him what no one else had managed to say, and now he had an inkling of why they called her the sage. He could still be a mimic and indeed he should be, she advised. No more of his time should be wasted, flailing about with indecision over what he was, for it was abundantly clear. "That's who you are," she said and she produced a fresh smile and for the first time that evening he smiled back.

She had confirmed that he had a skill few possessed. But truth be told he was more interested in hearing her expound on herself. She had something others did not have, or so he wanted to think, as she continued to extoll him. "Now show me how that other teacher speaks to his class," she said, laughing now and with a little glint in her eyes, something he just now noticed. Try as he might, he could not muster any fresh effort toward impersonation or anything of that sort, especially when his interest was her. This girl was different, he thought, and he deemed to know who she was and now he hoped she might tell him. Suddenly nearly every inhibition he had had with previous girls vanished with this one.

He reached for her hand. "I never heard a girl as beautiful as you," he started.

"Heard?"

"Yes. Your voice."

She blushed a little, though she kept her eyes fastened on him.

"Nobody ever told me that," she said, and she laughed a little.

"You must be an angel, I mean with that voice."

"Nobody ever told me that either, for sure," she said, and now her face blushed a little more. "Can we sit down?" she asked.

"Yes, of course." He motioned for her to take an end of the bench, while he stayed on the other. She looked at him quizzically at first and then presented a broad smile, the largest he had seen from her yet. He hoped it was genuine and he was not dreaming.

"I have wanted to talk to you for a long time," he said.

"It is rather nice to be thought of like an angel."

Suddenly he gasped, and the excruciating thought entered his mind that maybe he had expected too much from this girl, although he was not prepared to give up yet.

She held out two hands when he asked for one. "How about both?" she asked, laughing a little this time.

"Okay. I wanted to ask you if you have purpose in your life. With a voice like that you must." He felt desperation until she spoke again.

"Music."

"I see. That's nice. I have no ability in music myself."

"Perhaps I could teach you," she said, the glint in her eyes returning.

"I think I would like that. I mean the music . . . . And you. But I need to know what that beautiful voice issues from?"

"Well, Susan, Susan Winerod, but you knew that already, didn't you?" She looked at him quizzically.

"Yea, but I thought you might tell me more."

"More?"

"Yes, more."

"You might not be ready yet," she said.

He looked at her quizzically.

"You asked me about my mimic routine. I want to know where your beautiful voice comes from and I thought you might tell me. You know like our professor told us about Socrates and the liabilities of an unexamined life." Now he gently let go of her hand while the last flickers of any nervousness with Susan Winerod feel away from him completely and uncomfortably onto her.

"Well, there isn't much to tell, about me I mean. I simply open my mouth and the sound comes out."

He looked disappointed. "But that voice. It's even prettier than your gorgeous face. Surely you have some idea."

"I haven't had a man who could hold my hands as nicely as you just did."

"Thank you," he said, disingenuously. He did not desire a compliment; he wanted to know her and now she seemed unwilling, or worse, incapable. "So, you are simply a conduit for that beautiful way of speaking and expression." A painful look now spread over his face for he dreaded further conversation with her, for he had no desire to hurt or humiliate her nor even to disappoint her hope of him. He continued, nonetheless. "Are you like the poet Ion before the inquiring Socrates; you have no ideas about your gift or how it comes into your possession? You simply use and enjoy it?"

"You're sounding like our teacher, but I have to go soon. Tomorrow we can talk more over dinner?"

He looked startled. "You're taking me to dinner?" he asked.

"No, you're taking me, silly!" she said, with sly expression and an uncommitted smile.

"I don't understand. Well, okay. I mean certainly. Yes, that would be welcome." He looked disappointed, again.

"But for now let's finish today." She looked squarely at him, seemingly undeterred and undaunted by what he had just said to her. Meanwhile, he sat stiffly until she leaned over and planted a kiss on his forehead and then she pulled back just enough to square her mouth with his. She pulled him close and moved forward with her lips toward his and kissed him and then pulled away.

"By tomorrow I will have had sufficient time to tackle your little question," she said. "Perhaps I can glean a bit of answer from those burdensome books our teacher expects us to read for his class. I only pretend to have interest," she said. "And it goes a long way," she continued.

"Do you pretend with other things?" he asked.

"Depends," she answered.

His head dropped as low as it had been on their previous walk. "I may not need dinner," he said.

She blushed a little. "Why is that?" she asked.

His head rose back up. "I fear you're like the rest of them," he said.

She paused and starred at him and then looked away before she spoke, her smile finally given up as she turned back to face him.

"And what's wrong with that handsome? In answer to your question, yes, I'm a quieter and smarter version of the others, but they're not so bad. They know how to live. Some people don't even know how to do that because they're too busy readying silly books and asking silly questions and acting silly."

The supplicant got up from the bench and walked away. The sage still had time to make her eleven o'clock appointment and did.

10

The Hussy

"Seeing you is worse than last time!" she shouted, with flailing arms and slinging a cane across the room as she plopped in a chair to catch her breath.

He stomped across a splintery den floor and returned the insult while he fumed at the woman now sitting in the hard chair in one corner and breathing hard with her weak hand over her strong heart.

"Seeing a man in your wayward condition is never pleasant," she said, her voice strong enough to match any bluster of her son and adversary.

After another insult, Harold Broussette turned around to the woman slumped in her chair before he stormed out and said no more. The slammed door shook windows in a dwelling twice the age of the occupant and short on structural integrity with termites and inferior construction most everywhere. The woman's closed eyes suddenly opened and she pulled herself up in the chair. She noticed she sat alone again.

Harold walked, almost ran, back to his car. He knew his fight with one woman would surely provoke a fight with the other—though neither woman had seen the other yet—except in photographs. He would not entertain the subject of his mother anymore with Petulia Crimson. The rider sitting in the car must go with him or fend for herself on this forsaken soil, though Harold feared he could not bluster the younger woman as he just had his mother.

"Sinning always brings on suffering. And the Apostle Paul says death too. That girl is blinding you to the ways of evil, but yous too frail to see it. A man ought not to be with a woman till he's forty at least, or till he's got some sense, whichever comes first. A boy liken you ought not to be with a woman at all, probably. Your Papa was forty four when yous was born. By that time the man had sense enough. God rest his soul. I'm grateful he's not alive to see you still lacking any improvements in yourself."

Harold's mother had sat down in her only soft chair to finish her rebuke of her son, speaking in a moderate tone this time with only her ears to hear her words.

Petulia had stayed in the car, parked a few hundred feet or so from the house, where she heard nothing discernable in the crossfire of words except the occasional very loud swear word, and that undoubtedly from Harold. She knew Harold had already calculated the wasted sixteen minutes with his mother in his head before he reached the car and her. The demons of time and money had extracted more from him again.

"The old biddy has no sense left. I mean she never had any to begin with. Only now she's more repulsive than ever," Harold shouted to Petulia. He need not have. A couple feet separated the two bodies sitting in the front seat. He ignored his seat belt as he permitted the car to roll forward.

Petulia grabbed the steering wheel. "Stop! I didn't come this far for this. I wanted to meet this woman; that was part of our agreement!" Petulia protested with a voice as commanding as Harold's was weak. He waved his hand dismissively while the car started to move again. He swore a word or two and then spewed viler words while he accelerated the engine in his stopped automobile.

"I asked for a few minutes with her."

"Very well. Be my guest!" he shouted as he braked the rolling car to less than a comfortable stop for her.

"I'm not going back in there!" he shouted.

"Do I get more than ten minutes?" Petulia mocked, in derisive tone, knowing that now she would be finally relieved of Harold and his company for good. Petulia suddenly reached out her right hand and slapped his sulking face hard. "We had an agreement," she said, "and you broke it. Don't expect to hear from me again, just my lawyer," she continued.

While Harold sulked with pretended injury, Petulia zipped down her pants to tuck in a dangling shirttail before she zipped back up and flapped down the visor mirror to check her flush.

"Any beauty you presume possessing won't be anything of the sort to this woman, so no need to waste it on her!" he warned, still holding the side of his face.

Petulia slapped the face again. "The woman has a head for something. Maybe not for me. I'll see about that with no thanks to you." She said each word with as much sarcasm in tone as she could muster and got out of the car and slammed the car door harder than Harold had slammed the door to his mother's house.

"You've got ten minutes!" he shouted after her.

"Don't wait up," Petulia said over her shoulder. She did not bother to look back and resisted her natural inclination to pity pathetic creatures. She walked toward the path of the ramshackle house with relish, knowing she had Harold's eyes and so she stood under the shade of Spanish moss and the leaves of giant water oaks for annoyance. She took out the picture of his mother he had given to her on the trip down and studied it again. The photograph evidenced a face of somberness, but surely there must be more to the woman she considered. Perhaps the woman had had too few happy days in her life, the lack undoubtedly due to son Harold, Petulia reasoned. Petulia heard his "two minutes" shout, the infuriating but pathetic figure still under the illusion she might go back with him. She now she turned her attention away from the photograph and him and toward a house less that eighteen inches above waters of the bayou. An unleveled and hand-painted sign hung to the left of the entrance door. "Welcome," the sign said. That was more than what she had felt with Harold.

"Didn't stay for you did he honey?" The accelerating automobile and squealing car tires caught the attention of both, though neither woman bothered to look out through smoky windows.

"Nothing to worry about," the thirty-three year old blonde said, every word tinted with warm anger. The house inside looked little better than the outside, though it proved interesting enough to Petulia that she put away recalling the prior episode with Harold. The old woman had come to the door when her visitor first knocked and even politely held the screen door open. She told Petulia, who had introduced herself to her hostess first, that her name was Monwhat. Harold had ridiculed his mother's name to Petulia their entire road trip. "Good riddance," Petulia said silently, though she castigated memory for permitting the recollection of him.

The two women sat quietly for a minute before Monwhat explained that her unusual name came to her because her unwed mother, named Celia Freshbin, had initially heard the name pronounced and spelled incorrectly. Because two years of age was too late to change a child's name, that name being the sound the child answered to, the child Monwhat had been stuck with the name for seventy two years. She didn't mind the oddity anymore and actually never really had, she said.

"Peoples gets used to about anything anyways if'n you gives them time enough. Them that hears it a lot don't evens think it's so unusual a name or funny anymore. Sometimes children ask me about my name and they express interest for a while," she said. "I understand their surprise, because I never met nor even heard of another Monwhat."

The woman had clear and evident pride, though son Harold's cataloguing of his mother's failings and his unending complaints against the woman who brought him into the world gave no indication. After an uncomfortable minute Monwhat told her guest that the young woman was showing too much of her flesh unless she desired the kind of men desiring the flesh more than the nicer things belonging to females.

"I expect my boy weren't really interested in you, just your material," the woman said as she glanced in the direction of the young woman. Despite such forthright words, Monwhat seemed hesitant to look at Petulia directly, though the old woman offered her tea at the next lag in their conversation.

"Thank you," the younger woman said, "I'm a little exhausted from that fight with your son at the car, so that would be good."

"Lover's quarrel, was it?" Monwhat inquired.

"No. No love, none. Just all quarrel."

"I see. Would you mind fetching the tea for us? My right leg doesn't always work as it should. Plus I'm still a little short of breath from that encounter with my earlier visitor."

"Certainly." Petulia noticed two canes in the room, one lying in a corner, before she got up.

"Go through the sliding glass door to the deck outside and open the tin box sittin' down in the water. Fetch the glass gallon jug inside. It's about half full, so not so heavy.

And while you're out there, see if my wire fish trap, right next to the tin box, has got any fish," Monwhat explained.

Petulia found the tea jug, and when she came back, Monwhat took the container to a kitchen filled with windows, though any sun was shaded by mature water oaks outside. Monwhat pointed to the softer chair for her guest. The old woman prepared the tea for drinking in plastic glasses and with an occasional and furtive glance at her guest that Petulia could not help noticing.

"No fish?" Monwhat asked.

"I'm sorry. I forgot to look. I'll check." Petulia repeated her steps and returned with a report.

"Two fish," she said.

"Thank you. I may do em for supper for you and me in a little while. Made that trap only a week ago, tried it in different places, but this one is in the best place for catching and easy to attend to, being right here at the house. I got extra bedding for you. It ain't much, but it'll get you to daybreak anyway, I mean if you'll spend the night and yous more than welcome. Truth is I don't have much company down in these parts so I do like folks to visit. That boy of mine I hadn't seen for nearly two years until today. I knew what I could expect, so I don't really know why I invited him. But I did anyway. He presented no improvements over his visit two years ago. Frankly he was worse. He's got no sense, only money sense, I mean if that counts for a kind of sense. Naturally when I seen you walking down the path I figured he might be attracted to you for your figure—and for all I know you might be accommodating him," the old woman continued.

Petulia ignored the suggested association and instead complimented her hostess on the sweet tea. "Good stuff," she said and Monwhat looked straight at her guest this time.

"My own recipe, known only to me," she boasted. After the exchange the two sat in silence for about a minute, though neither now seemed to mind.

"If'n you'd go to church with me in the morning, I'd be much flattered and you'd be much welcomed. We'll take my boat, and with two people to paddle, we should be there in about twenty minutes. By myself it takes me about a half hour. And I can always use an extra hand if'n I have to do any shootin' along the way. I mean cause of snakes and maybe a wild hog," she said.

Petulia could not remember seeing a snake anytime during her lifetime except behind glass in a zoo and never any wild hog anywhere. She wasn't for sure certain that she had ever even seen a domestic hog, the kind that end up on the human eating table. She had spent the immediate past four months in urban and cultured Paris, and though time in that great city sounded glamorous and her trip envious to most, Petulia was tired of her work, mentally and physically, but mostly mentally. She told her boss to plan no more extended business trips for her for at least another year after she arrived back six days before the road trip with Harold. Sensing that Petulia had no inclination to compromise at this point, Petulia's nervous boss, after listening to a half hour of Paris stories from her with no bearing or relevance to her tremendous volume of sales, offered her a partially salaried leave of absence and that before he handed her a cup of strong coffee. "For a job well done in Paris," he said. "As for the time you'll be on leave, you can be building up your stash of skill to sell even better—I mean if that is possible!—when you come back." Petulia was quite unenthused by the word sell or the activity of selling at all right now, though she needed no persuasion to accept the offer of leave. Wanting to make certain of a definite deal with her, Petulia's boss threw in a not immodest expense account for the duration. "And no receipts will be necessary," he added, trying to present his offer to her as more than generous. He shook her hand heartedly after he finally received a slight smile from his pampered employee. He was convinced that for now at least he had prevented her from possibly leaving the company.

Petulia was hands down the most effective salesperson the company possessed and had been for almost five years. That fact was likely the only reason Harold Broussette knew who Petulia Crimson was because the man lived in an introverted world of his making. The same afternoon that Petulia made the rounds of visitation with her favorites in the office, she overheard Harold loudly lamenting, at a distance of thirteen cubicles from her own roomy office, his dread of an upcoming visit to see his mother. Petulia was never asleep in any of her surroundings and she immediately heard the word bayou. The fact that Harold, who was very unlikeable at a distance and less so up close, found his mother impossible was a positive clue for Petulia to his mother, for the young woman also never took such an assessment from such a source at face value. For Petulia, however, the overriding lure of any possible trip was mention of Louisiana bayou country. And, she might have occasion to practice her French, if it still lingered at points in the bayou. She heard Harold say at least three times that afternoon, in his own unsparing words, how he hated both the place and the person of his mother and most everything associated with either. Like any skilled salesperson Petulia now looked for opportunity and opening to seize what she wanted, for Harold presented blatant weaknesses making him easy prey to use. Indeed, he could be so inept as to presume he would be using her in any agreement, when it would be rather her game played, not his.

After ten minutes of talking—a mere third of the time her boss had talked with her—Petulia had a place in his car for the trip. Given her reputation in the company, Harold was deferential toward her, but no one, not even Petulia Crimson, escaped the voracious enthusiasm for money by this co-worker. Therefore, she would pay for her own meals and anything else like road tolls and she would pay for her own room when they stopped after the first day. Harold was so buried and busied in a life of careerism that he asked nothing at all about Petulia's real interest or motive in taking the trip. "He seemed only concerned that he had a paying passenger for our miserable journey down here," Petulia said to Monwhat. "So you could say I took advantage of him," Petulia said to her. "There was, however, nothing memorable about the two day trip of misery, until now I mean, so I can hardly feel any remorse for my maneuverings," she continued. Monwhat starred at the young woman uneasily.

The next morning produced no Harold, though neither Monwhat nor Petulia had expected any return. Nevertheless, during her night of poor sleep, Petulia had feared she had not seen the last of him and sat silently thankful for his absence as she gazed on the not small breakfast.

"I read my Bible at breakfast, always on Sunday and most other days when I can, unless I'm interrupted," Monwhat said, and she turned her eyes to her chosen Psalm while she pushed a forkful of hash browns down her mouth and urged her guest to do the same.

Petulia looked puzzled at first, but then asked if there was a book for her.

"If you desire it," Monwhat said.

"I do," the young woman replied.

"I'm sorry. I thought probably you didn't interest yourself in such matters—let me go and fetch one of my bestest," she offered.

"If it is any trouble, please don't," Petulia said.

"No trouble," Monwhat insisted, though this time she grabbed a helping cane.

The bed Petulia had slept in was beyond uncomfortable, for it was manifestly too soft, hardly more than a rectangular mass of unformed and ancient foam and possibly even some straw, Petulia conjectured. Every bit of weight of her slight body had plunged itself into the decrepit mattress while each knee had felt the hardness of the floor on every turnover during the warm night. The sound of singing frogs was nearly deafening at times, though delightful to her. Ten minutes after she rose from her sleep, she felt refreshed and wondered about the bed.

"Here you go," the woman said, handing Petulia an old Bible, and giving her a moment to find the Psalm. Monwhat began to read and after a few verses inquired if her guest wanted to read the final verses.

"Certainly," Petulia responded, and she dutifully picked up where the old woman had stopped.

The Psalm was short and after two minutes the young woman finished reading. Monwhat complimented Petulia on the fact that she stumbled on not a single word of the Psalm, not even the word Negev. For no particular reason, Petulia turned to the beginning pages of the Bible and found scribbled names and lined pages of neatly formed dates of births, deaths and marriages. Not wanting to appear nosy, she seemed anxious to hand the Bible back to Monwhat.

"I expect that was the first time you ever read out of the Book?" her hostess inquired.

Petulia turned the Bible over in her hands a couple times.

"Maybe. I mean I heard some of it read at a funeral once I think. Very pretty words," she said. "And you have a beautiful reading voice," she said also to Monwhat, though not entirely truthfully.

"I mostly taught myself to read. My folks weren't much for schooling, though I went a few years. My ma had only two years of school. I did like to read, though, and so my reading skills improved over time. My kids actually went to some college, though some more than others, but none for me or their Papa. Well, we've dotted long enough. Our breakfast is gettin' cold; we best attend to it."

Petulia did not desist and ate all that was on her plate, even one thing she was unsure of until the sure taste of snails reached her palate. Her hostess smiled when she saw that the young woman might be the type to turn nothing away that Monwhat served. "One thing I hate is a grownup who's as picky as a fussy youngin' about what's on their plate for eatin. We'll have some hot tea when we git home from church," she explained." "In hot weather a hot drink will do wonders," she added. "That's a foreign truth to Yankees that don't understand how to deal with hot, either the kind outside us or the kind inside us." Petulia smiled, but hardly understood the difference, not yet anyway.

The young woman stepped into the wooden boat while Monwhat reached out with a steady hand from her seat to make the transition safer.

"I never been in a boat as small as this one," the young woman said, before calculating that she actually had never been in a boat, and corrected her misinformation to Monwhat. Neither had she ever been fishing or hunting, she told Monwhat.

"So never shot a gun?" her hostess asked, as she held the rifle and then the shotgun in full view of the younger woman and with the barrels pointed straight up.

"No. Where I come from people, Yankees I mean mostly, some look down on guns and anybody who owns one, even sometimes the police. It doesn't make much sense I suppose."

"It makes worse than no sense, because it's nonsense," her hostess exclaimed. "When snakes and varmints and people show offense, my guns backs me. Course snakes don't think like people sometimes do; but the slithery creatures pay for their ignorance when their head's blowed off the rest of their offending body with my gun. My guns is about as close to me as my Bible on most days," she said, pointing to the two Bibles that lay against each other in a small sack in the bottom of the boat. "I tell folks I have two lethal weapons against the devil," she said, touching the Bibles in her sack with her foot and still holding up her shotgun and rifle. "I thought about bringing an extra piece, but figured there's strength in numbers—I mean two of us—so I could dispense with an extra one this time. Usually I pack a pistol though, for shootin stuff up close."

Petulia smiled.

"Guns keeps the peace and bring home the meat," Monwhat continued, almost smiling as she rubbed the side of her rifle, but then she laid the gun down in the boat to take up both oars, and handed the shotgun to Petulia. "I's just imagined you might not have navigation skills, so I'll get us there and you can enjoy the ride and do any necessary shootin. I got shells down in the bag there if'n we need em."

The gait of their walk was easy and slow. "I hope the service was tolerable for you," Monwhat said after the two walked out of the church almost precisely at noon. Except for Petulia's uncomfortable night of sleep, most everything seemed restful, almost beyond her belief, like most things over the past hours.

"The service was very nice. Haven't been in a church in a very long time. My parents never went and never took my sister and me, except maybe for a funeral. They told us later that they did not want to frighten us by seeing or being around a corpse."

"But death is one of the sure things of life. Taxes being the other," Monwhat said.

"So I've heard. A friend in college invited me to her church a few times, but I never went on my own. I guess I'm just indifferent."

"We don't have that denomination down here. Not that I know anyway," Monwhat said, as she motioned Petulia to a bench beside the north side of the church. Berried holly bushes graced the side of the church and the back of the bench, but none of the prickly leaves reached their backs.

"I took Harold and his brother and their sister to this church. It did Harold no good, or so he says, and I can believe that when I see him like he was yesterday. Except he's to fault, not this place. He hates everything about his upbringing. Me the most, but the church too. He hates his brother and scoffs at his sister's bad marriage. He still hates his Papa, and that despite the fact that the man, God bless his soul, he's dead and Harold loathes him still. Matter of fact, the boy hates everything about these parts. Good thing he found somewhere else to go, I mean I guess."

"That's a lot of hate. Anger I mean."

"Yes, tis so. He does have that. Tell me what you make of him, my son Harold I mean. I'm past trying to figure him out."

"I don't know where to start," Petulia said.

"Start anywhere," Monwhat said.

"Okay. Well, for starters, he's impatient. Makes him difficult to get on with, I mean with other people. He has few friends I think, though he doesn't seem to like being much by himself either. I think that's mainly why he let me come along on this trip, though he paid next to no attention to me. Not that I wanted any from him. The friends he does have are mostly males. They seem to me a lot like Harold. The bond seems only interest in money. I mean it sort of holds them together but that seems about it. Their careers are an exercise in climbing higher to make more money."

"Does he have a house?"

"A large apartment."

"So you've been there?"

"Only for a company party once, maybe twice."

"You don't sound enthused."

"Nothing to be enthused about. The entire evening most everyone talked only shop. I go to parties to get away from work. I guess they live to work and they carry work with them wherever they go and that is that," Petulia said, as she shrugged and said nothing for a few seconds while she starred out at the oak and pine and dogwood trees that dotted the churchyard.

"There's something I gotta confess." Monwhat blurted.

Petulia looked startled at first, not at all certain about what this might be, though she finally got her words out, "You don't have to confess anything to me. Really, no need," she said, her words a little wobbly.

"Well, I need to. I didn't sleep well last night over it, cause it's embarrassing. I'd feel better if I got this off my chest."

"I'm sure it's nothing too bad and you really don't have to . . . . ."

"Well, the thing is that Harold was mad at me when he stormed out of the house yesterday and for sure what I said to him angered him, so I bear some fault for what happened to you later, I mean all the shouting coming from the car. What I said was not very nice to him, but what I said about you wasn't any more kind. When he showed me a picture of you, I told him that his baser appetites were causing him to fall into sin even more than he is already stuck in living a life without God. . . but I said these things to him about you that I shouldn't have. Some of them he maybe didn't hear because there was so much hollerin and the like, but God heard them, so I'm accountable for them."

"I'm sure they weren't so bad, Monwhat."

"I wish I could say that young lady, but I can't. I called you a floosy, a hussy to Harold's face! Our conversation was so heated I was throwing everything at him I could think of, including words like that. Truth is, I hoped to drive him away from you, though more truth be told, I figured in my heart of hearts that he was the real problem and not you. I mean I wasn't really thinking about you as the real culprit. But I was thinking he was a sinnin' in a fleshly way with you and that by his own choice."

"We are—were— hardly more than acquaintances. That was before, before we made the trip down here. And after what he did yesterday I think even less of him now than I did yesterday, which was lower than the day before. But Harold never laid a hand on me and I wouldn't let him even if he tried anyway," Petulia said.

"Good for you," Monwhat said and she lifted her head up a bit.

"I came with him only because this place sounded interesting, but mainly because he spoke so ill of everything.

His view of the world and people is so upside down it made what he said more than a little fascinating to me. I actually thought it might be a little bit of the opposite, paradise, or something like that."

"A fine place it is here," Monwhat said, "but there is no paradise found in these parts," she continued, her face as serious and glum as any face Petulia had ever seen, except maybe the picture Harold had given Petulia.

"I understand, but you see I feigned a deceptive interest to get here. It was because I wanted to see the place. Frankly he hardly noticed I was in the car with him most of the way."

"What's 'feigned?'"

"Pretended, made up."

"I see. So my son, depraved as he was, is, was not sinning with you?"

"No. Your son, please don't take offense, is more or less a child. From what I've seen of him he might be incapable of a real grown up relationship with another human being. I'm sorry to be so negative about him. And I didn't mean to be so blunt. I'm sorry."

Monwhat dropped her head again and now seemed at the brink of tears. Petulia put her hand on the older woman's shoulder.

"Monwhat, if I may, Harold might be a suitable mate for somebody, even though he's got nothing it seems but gobs of money on his mind and those are gobs he hasn't yet managed to get into his pockets or his bank account. On the way to your place and for three hours before we got here he talked about absolutely nothing but money and success in acquiring money. Finally, I asked him if I might turn the radio on and he didn't even hear me enough to say yes or no. So I turned it on anyway and with volume enough for me to hear it over his loud talking and still he did not notice me or the radio. He's like a small boy playing with his toys and oblivious to the world around him. He's an introvert in the worst kind of way."

"Maybe you could teach him to give a thought to bigger things, or maybe have just a little light-heartedness. Maybe to be a little like you."

"Monwhat that is too kind a thought, but thank you. He would be a tough case for anybody. To have love for somebody who doesn't love you back, like you do for Harold I mean, is astounding. My heart aches for you, it really does."

"Maybe you can teach him something. He lacks so much, though I know it sounds . . . ."

"I don't think that is possible with him, not right now, anyway, and not with me. Somebody else might be capable, but hardly me I fear. He's unteachable mostly because he's impenetrable. Things that might move most people I don't think move him at all. Not a mother who truly cares about him, not the lack of real friends apparently, not a sunrise or a sunset apparently, maybe not even pulling a fish out of the inviting waters here in the bayou—unless it was a paying fishing tournament!" Monwhat laughed a little with the last example, as Petulia continued. "I don't know who could jolt him out of his obsession with stuff he seems to think is the end all of life. Maybe your God," she said.

"He doesn't believe anything about God or even that there is such a being. Tells me that every occasion he gets, just to hurt me I figure. I think if anybody could approach him, it might be you," Monwhat said, feebly trying again. "I know you've disowned him since yesterday and I understand—believe me I do."

The young woman dropped her head and for a moment Monwhat feared she had said too much. There was a prolonged silence of about a minute until Petulia put her hand on Monwhat's shoulder again.

The older woman looked up. "Let's forget about that for a while, for a while anyway."

"Good morning ladies!" the male voice boomed in the background as the man walked across the church yard and toward the two women. Petulia recognized him as the minister.

"I have not had the pleasure of your acquaintance Miss," he said to Petulia reaching out his hand.

"Petulia Crimson," she said.

"Rev. James Broussette. You can call me Jimmy. Pleased you could join us this morning," he said, but then he excused himself to return to the church building. "I need only a minute," he said and he took off running.

"This is your son?" Petulia said to Monwhat, in disbelief that the man in the pulpit was Harold's brother. Petulia turned her head in time to see Jimmy racing up the back steps of the country church.

"I have a daughter, married, living in Oklahoma. She only minimally keeps up with me. She won't pick up the phone to call me, or almost never does and she usually hangs up when I call. Does write me a letter about twice a year. It's a good letter if she can keep the profanity out of it, which is the case with about every other letter, or one a year. Of the three, Jimmy is my best hands down, though don't tell the other two. I made that mistake a few years ago. They're hugely jealous of their younger brother, but they pretend other reasons. For one thing, they're envious of his good looks, but for a lot more too."

"Like what?"

"He's very pleasant. Neither his brother and sister are and in fact would not know how to be pleasant," Monwhat answered.

"What made him a preacher, I mean besides his looks?"

Monwhat smiled furtively.

"Jimmy could have done anything. He can do anything still and does. Unlike his siblings, he was not ashamed of where he came from or me and certainly not his dad. He saw his older siblings stumble and fall down through their high school years when he was in middle school. That's when adolescent Jimmy woke up and became a young man with some self direction. He brought me and his papa a single sheet of paper when he was thirteen with a written-out plan for his life. Two hundred and thirteen words. I remember, because he announced the number before he handed us the paper to read. Brought it to us the evening after his brother was cited for being in possession of illegal fireworks and then a week later for drag racing on a public highway. Two weeks earlier Jimmy's sister had been charged with underage drinking and six months later she was charged and convicted of shoplifting. A month after that she was convicted of breaking and entering and spent three years on probation for it.

Jimmy kept to what he scribbled on that single paper except he had indicated there he wanted to be an agricultural engineer. Had hopes of inventing a perpetual motion machine even and he did draw a lot in the evenings and in time acquired patents on a couple things, but he ended up studying for the ministry."

"How did that happen?" Petulia asked.

"I know partly because his papa took the boy to breakfast the morning after Jimmy's college graduation in agricultural engineering—Jimmy's heart's desire. When Clarence came to bed later that evening I asked him what Jimmy and him talked about, but Clarence could hardly talk at first. He became choked up, but said that was his grief over Harold and Mildred. He did tell me that he told our youngest that he should stay with the course he was on, but that God might detour him later for something else. I asked him what Jimmy said to that and Clarence said nothing, except that Jimmy thanked him. I wept a little myself on hearing that from Clarence. Then after two years of working in the field as a sales rep, which he was quite good at and made good money, Jimmy went to seminary. My Clarence was so proud of him. So unbelievably happy to have a son follow him in the pulpit. It was a pity that Clarence died before Jimmy got a church in this parish."

"Your children are the children of a minister?"

"Yes."

"But Jimmy . . . . He seems happy, I mean what little I just saw."

"He is. When he is not attending to his congregation he writes stories, mostly short ones and works on more inventions, the one of past years was a strawberry picker. Some simple fish traps he invented and those he is still perfecting and hoping to start up a company to manufacture them. But telling a story is his first love and telling people about the love of God through Bible stories and our stories is his real gift. It is one gift that makes him a powerful minister even in these backwoods of the bayou, because it ain't paradise in here all the time, but people like to hear him and most of them will listen. The ministry nor writing pay very well, so he does a little commercial fishing with three cousins, for income supplement. Two of them were ushers in the service today. He's been writing his second novel for about three years now, tells me he needs about another three to finish. Tells me if he had not grown up here and in my and his Papa's house, he would have nothing nearly as interesting to write about in the book he's writin' now."

"You didn't mention a wife?"

"Nor do I to him. He mingles some with the ladies, so I hear and sometimes see, but not very much. But I try not to ask. Best to keep out of your children's romantic lives unless they offer."

"So he is your best?" Petulia asked again.

Monwhat dropped her head and looked like she wiped one eye with a shirt sleeve.

"He's grateful, simple as that, and that's what makes my Jimmy a joy to me. He's happy for good and right reason and he's not hard to figure, like his brother and sister. They are consumed by their anger and jealousy. He doesn't resent things that his brother and sister resents about their childhood and their loathing of a parent that was a backwoods preacher.

Jimmy was and is proud of his father. Speaks to me often of him."

"Could he teach me a thing or two?" Petulia asked.

Monwhat kept her head down and said nothing this time. She did look up when Petulia spoke again.

"Because I need something. I sort of ran off from my job. I got time to find something else, maybe someone who could help me figure me out."

"If yous serious he might be able and willing. If you listened to his sermon this morning you know what I mean. He is capable and generous."

Rev. Broussette returned with a smile and cut flowers from the church altar, zinnias and snapdragons.

"For you, Miss," he said, handing them to Petulia in a painted vase and then offering to carry the vase.

"Mother, will Miss Crimson be joining us for lunch at your place?"

Monwhat beamed a sly look of pleasure. "Of course. Let's get in the boat and see if we can find something on the way to take home for lunch," the older woman said.

Petulia failed to find a stable boat bottom as her upper torso twisted from inept high heels until Monwhat's son extended a hand for safer maneuvering. Pleased as she was, she shuddered a little over the thought of what might lodge on her plate for lunch. There were no shudders over Jimmy.

11

My Brother's Keeper

"It'll be fire all over, not water like the first time."

"Nobody will believe that fire business. People quit talking that way after they figured out things like the plague were because of rats and rainstorms because of atmosphere."

"They didn't believe the waters of the flood were coming either—until they drowned in them. Too late when your nostrils and your lungs is full of water," Louis said.

"You got a way with words, Louis, deceitful words though they are," Clifford replied, almost smiling.

"So I been told, but I can talk till I'm blue in the face to people like you Clifford. If you aren't prepared to repent, it's all for naught."

"So you'll quit the harangue with me? I would be grateful."

"God offends most people, including you I know, because you been telling me that for a week now. You think God should mind His own business and that your business—I mean that their life—is none of God's business. You don't care for being told the truth about yourself, when it's a little unsavory I mean."

"Yea, that's right. That's why you never got anywhere with me with your religion. I don't like being bossed by you or that tag along god you've got with you."

"I see, but what you gonna do now Clifford? You can't live up in that drafty contraption in that tree for the rest of your life? Frankly it reminds me of a play pen, I mean the kind kids have, except its up in a tree."

"Maybe I can live in it."

"But what you gonna do?"

"Don't ask me stupid questions."

"Ain't you gonna talk to me anymore?"

"Nope, and quit bothering me. I need to rest a little. Climbing up to that tree is work."

"Clifford, you got no real home. Furthermore, that house in the trees will be burnt like the rest of everything. Look with your own eyes."

Clifford could see and smell the smoke, but it was just farmers burning crop residue from their fields, not any apocalypse when the world was supposed to go up in smoke, like Louis imagined.

Clifford was one of those people called "no count." Louis told Clifford that he was a product of the times the two lived in, and while Clifford couldn't be excused for his behavior, he wasn't to blame entirely for all his shortcomings. Louis also told Clifford that Clifford had no motivation for the right things, but he did have motivation for the wrong things. The present godless age gave people little to live for besides money, sex, and food. When Louis said things like that, he sounded most like a preacher to Clifford and Clifford hated preachers, but he tolerated Louis for the sake of some company.

Clifford rarely talked to Louis much about his past, except to complain that he was introduced to religion from the family who raised him because they were ignorant and tried to make him like them. When both of his parents died, Clifford was some distance away and found out too late to attend their funerals, but he told Louis he wouldn't have gone anyway. Louis's mouth dropped when he heard that, though he had said nothing. Clifford had two younger siblings, brothers, though they had cut off all communication with Clifford earlier when his odd ways started to push him away from his raising and them. Not long after severance of all family ties, he became a drifter of sorts.

Committing about three years to random wanderings over no less than about ten states, Clifford decided to try his home area again after that, though no one knew why, though he did tell someone that the trip was to see if the religiosity of the people had diminished. Word of his plan to return did get out—no one knew how—but no one knew where he was hold up and figured he was possibly moving around to avoid detection and harassment and sometimes he did have to move from one place to another to avoid hostilities of various sorts. With quite a few abandoned houses in the area, some folks suspected him of making use of some of them for a dry place to sleep.

When spring came, however, and with a roof not being quite as necessary as in winter, he quietly asked permission from a landowner if he could domicile in the corner of the man's woods. The landowner, who was distantly related to Clifford's family agreed to the request, but insisted on a very small spot in the remotest part of the woods, but even this distance was not removed enough from ne'er-do-wells who began to taunt the newly returned Clifford. When his patch of ground was located, and that meant only his lean-to, infiltrators ransacked everything and after another day he migrated to another place, but left a simple note of "thanks" on the landowner's front porch, signed with his "x," for Clifford had dropped out of school in the eighth grade and could barely read or write. After a few more weeks nobody saw or heard where Clifford Delaney might have gone. That was when Louis Cochrane stumbled upon Clifford in some woods adjacent to his last domicile and found him tying tree limbs together and constructing a hidden tree house almost thirty feet in the air.

Delaney's exterior had so hardened from reactions to his offending personality that he claimed to not even notice he had been forced into being a loner. Furthermore, Delaney's pride was such that he would not admit, not even to Louis, that he desired friends.

"I've lived without God, I can live without His people," he boasted to Louis, though Louis surmised that Delaney was not as content or as self-sufficient as he presumed, though Delaney's short temper forced Louis to keep such thoughts to himself most of the time.

"You ain't angry bout it?" Louis asked, as he brought some pieces of scavenged wood for the evening fire.

"Angry about what?"

"That you don't have a friend in the world?"

"No, like I told you before."

Louis would ask no more questions, for now.

"How much more wood we need?" Clifford finally asked, wanted to avoid the prior subject.

"We'll need a lot more than this," Louis said, and he pointed to a pile of tree limbs and brush off in the distance. "Lot more there," he said. "It's not just for dinner or the night. It's for burning the ground around us before the fire reaches us, so that it stops before it gets to us. God will take us through that fire if we repent of our waywardness," Louis said as Delayne's mouth dropped.

"You never give up on that bit of nonsense Louis?" Delayne almost got up to strike Louis across the face, but could not motivate himself enough to do it. Instead Delayne wondered why any God, real or unreal, would create such an idiot message as Louis spouted, though he would cease to try to answer that question after Louis left the next morning.

That night Louis insisted to Delayne that the loner needed to find friends, and more friends than just one.

"If you could do that, you might have more chance with your life and other people and God."

"Shut your trap Louis! What do you know about anything?" Delayne asked.

"I know a few things," he said.

Those were the last words of Louis Cochrane recalled the next morning when Clifford felt no pulse for a body still providing some warmth to the ground beneath.

Clifford Delaney refitted some of the stouter limbs of a lean-to into a drag sled. He placed the corpse face up, but Delaney had no sheets or anything that could serve as a covering for the deceased, so at about noon, he placed his own and sweaty shirt over Cochrane's head and upper torso and began pulling the sled barefoot and shirtless. Delaney had fastened to the sled a cup water and shoved two old orchard apples he found into a trouser pocket. He climbed back up to his tree house for his sixty four dollars, all the money he had, before leaving. He had not kept a wallet for the past four years.

He had only one stream to cross and he made good use of the occasion. Not sure Louis had ever been baptized, and while Clifford was not one to abide by theological contentions of any kind, he thought it only right to respect the beliefs of the dead, and out of proper respect for Louis he submerged the entire sled and corpse with it underneath the water. The shirt over the corpse almost floated away during the exercise and when Clifford retrieved the garment he made the Louis's hair a little more presentable before covering the chest again.

He sat on the creek bank afterward for rest before noticing a small nook where three fish paused for smaller fry, while Clifford prepared to extract a meal from the community of three. He reborrowed his shirt from the corpse and tied the clothing in such a fashion to make a net easily trapping two of the fish inside the garment. With the number of years he had spent on the land, Clifford was desensitized to the rawest of conditions for most everything, and he gutted the two fish with a razored edge rock and ate the main portion of the fish flesh raw, except for the head. The shirt was put back over the corpse.

In two hours he would stop for the night and build a fire to keep mosquitoes from stealing any blood of the corpse. As the fire blazed, Clifford reminisced over Louis's fantasy of a smoky end of the world, but tonight Clifford could not laugh nor mock. That failing, he tried to recite the beginning verses of Psalm 51 because Louis read them every night for the few nights they had been together. Clifford usually insisted Louis stop with the reading, however, especially after verse eight. Now, Clifford wept that his transported corpse had no verses to utter for him and he could remember none of them.

Clifford Delaney would have preferred crossing the moistureless Death Valley with a shriveled corpse than having to endure onlookers as the shirtless and barefoot man drug the sled into town the next morning. He asked the first person he saw for any undertaker in town, fearing that he might have to go further afield to find one, but his luck was rewarded and one came to him, after word got out. The day was unfortunately Saturday and people from every direction and quarter gawked at the spectacle of the deceased on Clifford's sled. The undertaker, a man of late middle age, hurriedly sent a youngster back to the undertaker's business for a covering and in short time, Louis Cochrane's corpse was completely masked by a fresh white sheet. The shirt that had previously covered the head and upper torso of the corpse went back onto Delaney's living body.

"Bring the body to the back of my building," the undertaker suggested and Delaney nodded.

The undertaker and his young helper met Delaney and the corpse while each person exchanged furtive glances among themselves.

"We will place the corpse inside a bag and then we can go inside," the director finally managed to say and the youngster went to work. With the corpse in the black bag the director pointed to a table top and the three of them lifted the bag onto the table.

"Mr. Delaney, I believe it is?" the director asked.

"Yes. The deceased is Louis Cochrane."

"Will you be in charge of arrangements and payment, Mr. Delaney?"

A surge of perspiration from every pore of his warm body stalled any answer that Delaney might have given to the undertaker.

"Shall we confer in my office?" the undertaker suggested after waiting longer for an answer than he wanted.

"Yes."

"Please sit if you will," the undertaker instructed.

"Thank you."

"Mr. Delaney, are there difficulties regarding payment of my services?"

"At the moment, yes. I have a small sum of money, with me I mean. If more is required perhaps I can have credit for that, I mean if that is possible."

"Credit is possible. Do you have any credit history?"

"No."

"Well, how much money do you have, for the funeral and burial I mean?"

"I was thinking that perhaps we might just bury the body without a service. That would save some expense perhaps."

"Yes, that is a possibility and would save money. I suppose we might also dispense with embalming the corpse. However, if we do that we need to have the corpse buried by before noon tomorrow, maybe sooner."

"I see."

"When did the deceased die?"

"Sometime between midnight and 6 o'clock, yesterday."

"Then he must be buried before midnight tonight. And since funerals are not conducted in the evening, not in our area anyway, it must be today before sundown."

"That doesn't give much time. And I have not notified any family because I have no connections with his family."

"That's too bad, I'm afraid, but a quick burial must still happen. But there remains the item of the money, how much do you have, for the expenses of burial I mean? I must ask because without proper credit, I must have the money before the work."

"I have six hundred dollars, but most all of that a friend is bringing to me this afternoon, so I can provide it then."

"And that would not be the family of the deceased?"

"No, someone else."

"I see. Very well, in these circumstances and given the urgency of burial, I suppose I can wait a few hours for the money. I will take what you do have, however, as down payment."

"Forty dollars."

"Forty dollars! Is that it?"

"I am afraid so, Sir, my friend's death caught me by total surprise. I was not prepared for it and certainly not for the expense of a funeral."

"Well, it will hardly be a funeral. I mean I haven't buried a dead soul for such a price in the last decade! And if you have no other money, this will mean your friend will be buried without embalming, and in a cardboard box and with no marker above ground. Fortunate for you is that we have a pauper's field for burials like this. An officiating minister will still be provided, but he will speak no more than five minutes, probably less. And you will have to pay extra for a death certificate. If this is agreeable to you and if I can have your forty dollars, I and my assistant will get started on your friend. I suggest you go get yourself a decent set of clothes for the funeral, but if you have only the forty dollars, which I will need, I don't know what I can suggest to you. Perhaps my helper Claude can show you where we keep some trousers and shirts to bury people in. You might chose something in that stash, and it is complimentary, as long as you can return it after the funeral. And now if you will excuse us, we must get to work. You yourself be back here promptly by 3pm. It is 1pm now. Do you expect many attendees at the funeral, I mean at the graveside?"

Delaney dropped his head and when the director grew impatient with no answer, Clifford blurted out that he expected no attendees at graveside.

"That's a shame," the director said, exhibiting a slight bit of feeling that until this point in the conversation was nowhere to be found from the businessman, except in their very initial conversation.

"Perhaps I can send Claude out to enlist some mourners before then," he said, and Delaney nodded with thanks and with his head down.

"I will take a look at some of those clothes you mentioned," he went on to say.

"Certainly," said the undertaker, with a smile of sorts.

"Excuse my interruption," the man in clerical collar said, and Delaney twisted around to see the speaker.

"My sympathies on the death of your friend."

"How did you know?"

"The undertaker's hireling is broadcasting it up and down the streets."

"I see."

"Was he a close friend, I mean the deceased?"

"Yes, very. About the only friend I had left in the world. As bad as it is to lose him, I just committed a grievous wrong in the last hour. When the funeral is over I may be put in jail."

"May I ask why?"

"Reverend. I had sixty four dollars in my pocket when I came here today. I was afraid the undertaker would not do the burial for such a pittance, so I told him I had $660. I told him I only had forty dollars in my pocket—not true either—and that the rest of it would come today, after I handed him the forty. I came in here now not to remember my only friend—though I am naturally in grief over his death—but to ask forgiveness for such a terrible sin as I have committed. I'm almost glad my friend is gone, so he did not have to witness such a display of lies such as I just concocted."

"But you asked for God's forgiveness?"

"Yes, of course. But I have to do something about the rest of it—I mean claiming I am going to pay a debt I cannot pay."

"But you did ask for forgiveness?"

"Yes, as I told you. Is there something more?"

"Well, you might go and tell the undertaker what you have done and if he does not shred you with a shovel tell him you could work off your debt by doing some grave digging for him. He buries about a person a week. You might have to be here for some time to equal the amount you owe, though that would do justice to the undertaker, don't you think."

"Yes."

"But God forgives us with greater love than sometimes we can manage in forgiving one another. So, the undertaker, as you probably surmised already, may not be so quick to forgive, not like God anyway—or he might. What do you think?"

"I think I must go talk to the undertaker."

At three o'clock, as instructed by the undertaker, Clifford Delaney stood outside the funeral facility and waited for the doors to open. Suddenly the doors were thrown back and a moving carriage with a casket in its center was first pulled and then pushed by the undertaker and his helper Claude to a single horse carefully maneuvered into position to pull the carriage. A dozen yellow roses lay on the casket. The horse's tail was braided and the animal had a plume going upward on its head.

The director instructed Delayne to grab and hold the bridle of the horse from the left for movement to the burial site, and Delayne might have done the task any other time or day, but his tears became so profuse that the reverend offered to hold the bridle from the other side and the two in unison walked with the animal. Except for the noise of the clopping feet of the animal, there was no other sounds heard, though there was a horde of people joined in walking behind the hearse.

The pauper's field was an ample half mile from where the procession began, though none of the walkers seemed to show fatigue before the carriage stopped. A gentleman from the mourners walked up to the open plot to bring the horse and carriage alongside before he unhitched the animal and led the beast under a shady grove of oak trees before tying the animal off. Six men stepped from across the foot path and made their way to the grave and three from each side then hoisted the cardboard box off the carriage and to the open hole in the ground. With the casket now sitting above ground and ready for the downward journey into the earth prepared to receive her own, Clifford Delaney fell to his knees. The reverend bent over to say and hear words unheard by anyone else and after another minute he stood back up.

"Today we lay to rest the good friend of Clifford Delaney. Mr. Delaney most of you know, but none of you I think know or knew the deceased, Mr. Cochrane, Louis Cochrane. Mr. Delaney tells me that Mr. Cochrane was the last and only friend he had over the past couple weeks, but that he sincerely hopes to make some new friends in our town soon, for he shall be staying in our parts for a while."

The funeral director grimaced over this sudden announcement, but then forced a smile, for news travels fastest in small communities, and the reception of news, sometimes faster.

"Mr. Delaney too wishes to express sincere regret and sincere apology for how he has he has presented himself in the past toward us and he wishes to be forgiven. And on this particular day, he wishes to thank each of you for coming out to express your sympathy in his loss of his passing friend, Mr. Cochrane," the reverend continued. At this point, Clifford Delaney, who had until then had his back to the other mourners, turned around and gave a brief nod of thanks. Some of the crowd of mourners returned his nod.

When the ceremony soon concluded, after a reading of Scripture and prayer by the reverend, Delaney made his way to the undertaker to thank him for his services and to assure the man that he would start work the very following day, should he be needed for a grave digging that soon.

"I am afraid that will not be necessary," the undertaker said, somewhat wryly. "Your bill was taken care of today before the ceremony."

Shocked as Delaney was by such news, his mind went to other things.

"I shall be staying nevertheless," he said.

The undertaker put his hand out. "I am truly sorry about the death of Mr. Cochrane. I fear I have not had a friend as good as he seems to have been to you."

"I'll remember that," Delaney replied, as he reached out to shake the undertaker's firm hand.

12

The Sinkhole

Jasmine Scott could not, she insisted, mourn the passing of her prize bull before receiving authoritative pronouncement on the animal's untimely cause of death. The woman's ladies in waiting ambled about, voicing perfunctory agreement with their employer as they variously amused the woman sitting in her rocker and who had refused to grieve until the required information came forward.

"But he is dead, is he not Lady Jasmine?" one asked, fearing her lady was only delaying her grief for a suitable moment.

No response was forthcoming, just a landlady staring out a window at the willow tree in the south corner of an enormous yard.

"Perhaps I should take you for some proper mourning clothes?" another lady offered, though the suggestion only met with more expressionless gazing through the window at the willow tree.

"Perhaps you could assist me in making my way outside for some fresh air?" Jasmine suddenly opined. Though not quite successfully, she almost stood up from her chair, before she fell back on her purple seat cushion.

"Certainly," one of the three women said, while another fetched the woman's walker and another simply observed the commotion before feeling the floor slightly quivering in the main room of the house. The hurried excitement of carrying out an order from a woman who had not spoken the previous three hours detracted almost everyone from any notice of anything else. Save for Stacy, and only barely so with her, there was no expectation that catastrophe lay underneath the house, or that the house would soon be ripped from formidable foundations.

Once outside Jasmine Scott stepped off the downward ramp from her porch and onto friendly manicured grass before a swath of slumping and then collapsing ground in front opened up and the lady feel downward headlong, preceded by her walker. The quaking earth ripped an expanding hole of death of sufficient dimension to devour the first of Jasmine's three ladies in waiting. Named Christine Bunson, she had foolishly peeked downward in the hole too closely to the falling earth. There was a frightening scream by Christine when the earth gobbled her up, though no whimper nor any sound emitted from the ground afterward. It was a death made quicker than most could have imagined, least of all by people rarely venturing outside.

The remaining breathing women screamed in screeches of terror as they jockeyed about the portions of diminishing stable ground for any suitable havens of safety. There had been no drills practiced by the four women in preparation for such a catastrophe. Nature in their locality had been relatively benign for nearly the past century, with nothing that might be termed a natural disaster. Nothing like a sinkhole had appeared anywhere in the county for over a half century. Nonetheless, most of the yard closest to the house in only a matter of a few more seconds vanished, and what remained looked like a plowed field. The immediate thought of Stacy MacGregor and Ramona Cliff was that no ground was safe anymore and maybe their only possibility was escape back into the house until the two saw and then heard the frightful sound of cracking and shattered glass and then wood breaking apart with a screeching sound and then in a matter of hardly more than a half minute, the house, though still managing to stay in a single piece, slid downward toward the earth from its east side as some crusty foundation dangled in mid-air from the opposite end of the doomed structure.

Stacy and Ramona screamed in louder desperation at the sight of a fine house sliding into the earth and then each pulled free of the other's hand as they scrambled for the thread of hope of a still standing gigantic oak in the back yard. A ladder was necessary for scaling the tree, though neither of the ladies in waiting had climbed a tree nor even traversed anything except a two-step house ladder in the last decade. Furthermore, neither of the two were in any fit shape for the demands of such an occasion, even if they had had a ladder. Such conditions, however, were beside the point, for a ladder they would never have.

Ramona shouted her intent to visit a shed for the hopeful ladder, though the particular shed was out of sight from where they stood, so they had little idea if the building still stood. With the dangers of traversing anywhere at all on the yard, an argument began between the two over who should make the perilous hundred yard trek to the outbuilding for the needed ladder. After two minutes of arguing, blades of grass were drawn, and the unwelcome task fell to Stacy.

She undertook the dangerous exodus without complaint and was soon out of sight and headed to the hopeful shed, though she never came back, and Ramona never heard anything more from her, except Stacy's shout, right after she left Ramona, that she would quickly return. Ramona made visual and depressing survey of the catastrophe until the ground started to shake with more violence. In her fright, she managed to climb the tree without ladder and to perch on a tree limb until the trunk of the powerless tree became twisted and then uprooted, like the stately house at Forest Meadow.

The whole unimaginable scene might have been comedic for any passerby, given an upturned house jutting out of the ground, except for the fact that there were no witnessing neighbors that saw or heard the earth on the property sink, for neighbors were distant from the main house at Forest Meadow. The closest neighbor was a mile away and besides the distance, the resident there had not spoken to any of the four ladies in the past eight years. Beyond the absence of anything like community feeling at

Forest Meadow, except for Forest Meadow, the old woman Scott and her ladies in waiting were by design recluses. When closer neighbors might have been helpful for their predicament, no assistance was forthcoming because there were no close neighbors and least of all any friendly neighbors. All blame need not fall solely on the residents at Forest Meadow, however. With the main house as the closest thing to an English manor house to be found within a hundred mile radius, there was envy within the residences of other and unattractive houses that populated the area. More importantly, and a source of great agitation to the nearest neighbors, Jasmine Scott continued to own a vast portion of the original land purchase of her great great grandfather, Rutherford Nathaniel Scott, from almost a century previous. She had for years refused to sell even the tiniest portion of that land.

Nothing like envy for land concerned the hired women of Jasmine Scott as each hired lady had been handsomely and more than satisfactorily paid for their duties in exchange for their Madame's insistence upon essentially cloistered living with her over the past decade. Most employees would have balked at such a constrained environment for work, but each of the three hired ladies figured the old woman would die in about ten years anyway, though they hardly could have imagined the ghastliness of a hungry earth gobbling up their manor lady as the vehicle of her death.

Each of the three ladies in waiting was patiently enduring her probable ten years of toil in expectation that waiting would give the employee plenty in the end and probably sufficient means to never work another day afterward. Each of the three had, within the past six months reached forty years of age. Jasmine Scot had referred to forty as the best age for going out into the world with still some time, she insisted, for making a family. The old lady, too, had promised each hireling that if she remained employed with Jasmine at the time of the old lady's death, and not a minute less, a bonus of $100,000 would be theirs in addition to the already hefty wages from ten years work. The ladies in waiting had to muster a strenuous patience to free themselves of normal and tempting social relations, though as compensation, domestic finery and extravagant inside-the-house living had not been excluded. For allied reason, Jasmine had instructed in her document of legal will, a funeral so elaborate that her ladies in waiting surmised some land would have to be sold for the expenses. Indeed, her funeral would take on nearly the air of a state funeral, and that in the tiny county where Jasmine Scott resided at the lavish and secluded Forest Meadow.

Truth be told, Jasmine Scott, with her stories and papers and heirlooms and other belongings, would have been an historian's dream of an exquisite and unsurpassable treasure trove of history preserved, if she had allowed any such person even a glimpse. And, she might have, if her life had been different, that is, more rewarding, like she had hoped, rather than more disappointing, as it more often worked out. Raised in a family of near nobility as such was possible in southern America, she had married well, indeed very well, but the marriage did not give her what she had wanted most, for that was children. As if this want was not painful enough to endure, Jasmine suffered the loss of her beloved husband before the gentleman reached his sixtieth birthday and for nearly a decade she wore only mourning clothes on nearly every occasion requiring dress, both public and private. Moreover, there became less and less occasions where Jasmine entertained guests and increasingly fewer occasions when she went out at all. At the end of ten years living in such a manner, she decided to do something about her situation and set to work to bring to fruition new circumstances for a new life, or so she called the venture. Her accountant she called in first, so as to make sure she could financially do what she proposed. Though puzzled about the idiosyncratic nature of her plan, the accountant informed her that with her bulging assets should need hardly worry at all about money for her venture. With that green light given, she set to work.

She wanted women acting the part of adult daughters whom she never had, and that meant that Jasmine, now almost seventy years of age, would take in single women of the approximate age of thirty, and these women would have to be willing to delay their own marriage and children for ten years. As bizarre as the plan and intent behind the plan seemed, when word got out, Jasmine Scott had an avalanche of county and city women who eagerly clamored to vie for the positions. After some initial screening of candidates too many to count, ten women were interviewed from a pool of twenty. Five of the ten were selected for detailed screening and then further interviews. Aware that the hefty rate of pay and benefits could lure prospects solely for financial reason and that such persons could hardly always be infallibly excluded, Jasmine nonetheless scrutinized every factor or trait of every candidate she feared might compromise job performance.

The chosen women would be required to make their home at Forest Meadow. While each candidate must be single, one of the three could be a divorcee, but she must have no birth children nor step-children. While a university diploma was desired, it was not required but tutorials for two years would be available and required. A month's trial period or probation was required for the final five candidates for assessing suitability. If a candidate herself was still unsure, even if Jasmine was approving, the candidate could continue a second month in the same provisional capacity. After two months a final decision would have to be made between Jasmine and the candidate. Dating and courting would be permitted, but no more than once within one week and for not more than four hours outside of the house. Time spent on and around the property by the couple did not count for the four hours. In the event of an engagement, weddings must not follow earlier than six months from the day of engagement. The last three months of the engagement required the bride to be prepared for moving out by the wedding date. If desired, the married couple could take up free occupancy in one of Jasmine's tenant's houses for one year in exchange for full resumption of daytime duties in the main house at Forest Meadow. Many other rules, similar in nature, were part of the agreement drawn up for final candidate selections. Due to the unpredictability of such factors as engagements, and because Jasmine wanted no fewer than three ladies in waiting at any time in her house, she decided to begin her experiment with five women. Her chosen number turned out to be prescient, for in the third year one employee did get married and a second one in her sixth year of employment. The remaining three, Christine, Ramona, and Stacy, stayed for the duration, or until the incident of the sinkhole collapse brought catastrophic change and death to Forest Meadow.

The devastated property at Forest Meadow remained unobserved for a day, with the house stuck in the earthen sinkhole. On the second day the county sheriff, receiving an anonymous call that something was not right at Jasmine Scott's place, came out. No one was to be seen, not even when the officer resorted to shouting and then pulled his firearm out before sending a magazine of shots into the air. After some head shaking the sheriff left but returned with a sign condemning the property and a roll of tape he pulled around the entire area to warn and keep trespassers out. Before he finished, two of his deputies showed up, Caleb and Paul.

"What have we here?" Paul asked.

"Nothing the likes of which I've ever seen," the sheriff replied.

"Jasmine Scott lived here?" Paul continued.

"Yea. She had servants too. The whole set up was a little odd, to neighbors and most everybody else," the sheriff said.

"Deaths?" Caleb asked.

"Not sure yet," the sheriff replied.

"What a way to leave this world," Paul said, shaking his head.

"How about Stacy?" Caleb asked.

The sheriff and the other detective turned to Caleb.

"What about her?" the sheriff asked.

"She was one of Jasmine's three ladies," Caleb said."

"So four women lived here?" the other deputy asked.

"Four," Caleb said.

"How come you know something about this place," deputy Paul asked.

"I had gone out with Stacy on occasion."

"I thought old lady Scott frowned on that," the sheriff inserted.

"She allowed it with tight rules."

"I see. Did Stacy talk to you about her job here?" the sheriff asked.

"Sometimes," Caleb said.

"I heard the old woman kept the three under pretty tight wraps," the sheriff said.

"In a manner of speaking. But she paid them well. Stacy told me that more than once."

"I see. If I may say so, you don't seem very upset if she's dead," the sheriff said.

"Well, we weren't close, but she was decent company, though nothing special. She did talk a lot about the money she was expecting."

"Money? You've mentioned it twice now," the sheriff asked.

"Well, something about when the old woman died, each was going to get a big chunk of money."

"Well, for now we only presume she might be dead, like the others. We'll need four bodies to account for everybody I guess," the sheriff said. "Doesn't appear that any are in the house, but we'll see. If not, we'll have to go digging, I guess."

"So how do we proceed sheriff?" Caleb asked.

"First we'll need to raise the house up and get it out of the hole. Then we can examine everything inside. After that, dependent on what we find in the house, we'll go into the hole for whatever else may turn up down there."

The next day proved promising for the investigation. Before two cranes arrived at the devastation, Stacy MacGregor had been spotted staggering on a rural road almost six miles from Forest Meadow and was taken to the local hospital by ambulance. Hospital officials called the police station and within minutes the sheriff sat in Stacy's hospital room and subjected her to a round of questions about the incident at Forest Meadow. The first question revealed that Stacy had lost all of her memory and so the sheriff immediately radioed Caleb that Stacy had been found alive. When Caleb arrived at the hospital room, Stacy evidenced no recognition of him. Despite his best efforts to jog her memory of him she could muster no knowledge of him. He described in some detail the last date the two of them had had, where they had eaten and what they had talked about that evening during dinner. None of this information moved Stacy to any recall.

"There is no reason for me to doubt your word or your story, but is there any proof that relationship occurred, especially since Lady MacGregor seems to recall nothing," the sheriff said. Caleb appeared flummoxed at first until he picked up the room phone and called the police station. In a few minutes a female officer arrived from the station, and

Caleb whispered into her ear and then the female officer and Stacy went into another room at the far end of the hallway. In a minute or so, the two returned and the female officer nodded to the sheriff.

"Very well, thank you officers. Caleb, I'll need to see you a minute before we go," the sheriff said.

"Because of your prior involvement with Stacy—"

"Sheriff I only went out with her a few times, probably no more than three or so."

"Even so, you may be invaluable in our investigation, as will Stacy if her memory returns and particularly so if the other three women are dead."

"I understand," said Caleb. "I'll help in any way I can," he continued.

"Correct me if I'm wrong, but I think I have a memory of seeing you with a lady in town about a month ago, it was at the Roster's Rack restaurant I think. Yes, the wife and I stopped by to say hello at your table and you introduced her to us, I remember that now."

"Yea, that was Stacy. Like I said we had nothing special."

"I see," the sheriff said.

Even before the house was pulled all the way out of the sinkhole the back of a head and an attached arm were spotted down in the dirt. Caleb and Paul scrambled and managed to bring the body up with bones extruding from both arms and a smashed rib cage. Caleb immediately identified the deceased as Ramona Cliff.

"She was one of the ladies of the house," Caleb told the sheriff.

"You knew her too?" the sheriff asked.

"Not really. I mean I was just acquainted with her because of Stacy. The two were not the best of friends. They sort of tolerated each other I guess, though not all the time. According to Stacy, Lady Jasmine had to come between them sometimes."

"Sounds like all was not well in paradise out here," the sheriff said. "Anyway we have our work cut out for us. We've got two more bodies to come up with," he continued. "But maybe our first question is why Cliff's body was down in the sinkhole while Stacy was out walking around?" the sheriff asked.

"That's anyone's guess, I mean at this point," Caleb pitched in.

The crane operators had guided the salvaged house down onto stable ground while the sheriff and his deputies waited as the operators untied their cables and hooks from the house.

"It will take some work to get through all of that," Caleb said, as he tried to open one door of the discombobulated house and then another.

"Out here it looks like neither of the other two women are inside. I think we've got to get down in that mass of dirt and look there for them," the sheriff said.

Caleb continued to try the doors. "Wait a minute. The doors aren't just jammed, they're locked. But why are the doors locked?"

"This has the smell of foul play I think," Paul said.

"Go on," said the sheriff.

"Well, if you're scurrying to get out of a gyrating house, one that may collapse on you, you don't stop to lock the doors once out. You move away from it as fast as you can," Paul offered.

"But somebody did, I mean took the time to lock them," the sheriff said.

"Probably after it settled they went back in for something," Paul offered.

"Presuming the quake had stopped somebody could maybe go back in. But only a survivor could have done that and a survivor who had a key—or went back inside for a key," said Caleb.

"So that rules out Cliff. She's dead and we found nothing in her pockets," the sheriff said.

The sheriff sent Caleb to the hospital. A box of items from her clothing showed a key, and Caleb was about to return to Forest Meadow with the news and more questions, when Stacy stopped him.

"I thought you had come to see me," she said. Caleb paused while Stacy's expression stayed the same. "Could you have dinner with me this evening, I mean here in my room with me. I can make an order for you, if you can come. If you're eating at home alone anyway, then we could have one another's company, I mean if you want to," she said. They will just put it on my bill when I leave here."

Caleb paused for some uncomfortable minutes. "Yes, I suppose I could do that, but is seven too late for dinner? I have to talk to the sheriff a bit before I could be here and it may be that late."

"Seven is okay."

Caleb walked toward her and against his better judgment kissed her forehead, touching the back of her head with his cupped hand. He felt the soft tissue of a head wound, but she knew nothing about any incident. "Part of everything I seem to have forgotten," she said.

"They did look at this when they first checked you in?" he asked.

"I think so," she said.

When Caleb arrived back at Forest Meadow, there were two more bodies on stretchers covered with sheets and the coroner was present. The sheriff asked for autopsies on all three.

"Nothing significant in the pockets of any of them. Lady Scott did have a small crucifix in a shirt pocket," the sheriff said. "Lot of good it did her in her time of need," he added, shaking his head. "What did you find?" the sheriff asked."

"MacGregor had a key, but I found out something maybe as helpful as her having the key. She has a pretty sizeable gash on the back of her head, like something cut or slashed her. Though the wound seems on the mend, it was much more than a scratch or a scrape."

"I see. No idea how she got it?"

"No. Says she doesn't remember anything like that. It could be from something that knocked her unconscious," Caleb said.

"Is there more?" the sheriff asked, noticing his deputy's delay.

"Yes, MacGregor asked me to have dinner in her room in about an hour. I said yes thinking maybe she might reveal something about her part in all of this. I think though that she just wants some company right now."

"She may need more than your company when you tell her we have recovered three bodies from Forest Meadow," the sheriff said with a quizzical look on his face. "Did you tell her about finding Ramona?" he continued.

"In so many words," Caleb said.

"How did she react?"

"Nonchalant. But remember, she doesn't remember the woman, nor the other two. If she appears cold or indifferent, it is because she can't remember them," Caleb explained.

"Don't presume anything about the possible motives of this woman. I dare say none of us know her well enough for that," the sheriff interjected, seeming a little irritated at his best deputy.

"Sheriff, she may be romantically inclined toward me, particular after our interview with her at the hospital and what it revealed about her and me in the past. Though she remembers nothing of it, she may think she can pick back up with me."

"Perhaps, but when her memory comes back, her old self may come back with her."

"Well, she may be simply offering herself as helpful to us, though she is only along for a free ride, maybe to get me," Caleb said.

The sheriff laughed a little. "Excuse me for my chuckle. Perhaps she really does think you are her knight in shining armor and she is not going to miss her chance, no matter."

"It is okay, I mean our dinner?" Caleb asked again.

"Yes. I will see you in the morning."

"Understood."

"I am sorry for being later than expected. We had to wrap some things up."

"It's okay. I needed real company, not doctors or counselors. I need time with someone who knew me," she said.

"Has your day been good?" he asked.

She nodded, without any expression. "I am afraid your mashed potatoes may be cold. Shall I ask the kitchen to warm them for you?"

"That won't be necessary. They are fine, really," he said, smiling.

"Am I like what I was like before?" she asked, as she lay her fork down for his answer.

"Well, yes. Maybe you have more questions now. But that is understandable, your memory is blank and you want it back."

"Tell me more about me when we knew each other," she asked.

"Well, as far as us, we went out a few times. I particularly enjoyed one occasion, the time we walked around the property at Forest Meadow."

"The people here tell me here that I have traumatic brain injury," she interjected.

"So I've heard."

"I don't think I ever heard of that Forest Meadow place. You say I lived there?"

"That's where you came from, yes."

"It has a nice sound, the words I mean."

"It's also a beautiful place. You told me when we went out that it was pleasant to work there and that you were paid well."

"I don't remember that, I mean about the money. What else did I tell you about it?"

Caleb paused for a few moments. Stacy starred at him. "You told me Lady Jasmine had been kind to you."

"I don't think I know Lady Jasmine," Stacy interjected.

"She owns Forest Meadow."

"Is she doing well? I mean I hope she isn't worried about me."

"I don't think she is worried about you. You are in good care here, she is in good care where she's at," Caleb replied.

"Is she in this hospital?"

"No."

"If I could talk to her that might jog my memory."

"Perhaps," Caleb replied. "How is the gash on your head?" he asked.

Stacy reached behind her head. "Seems okay." "No more hurt?"

"It only hurt until yesterday, but not now."

"No idea how you got that laceration?"

"No, but I would like to see Forest Meadow. Do you think you could take me there?"

"We would have to talk to your doctors here. You don't think it might be a bit too soon and too much for you, I mean to go out there right now?"

"No."

"You seem anxious to see it."

"I'm anxious to see a lot of things. I'm just as anxious for you to see them, dazzling things, things not just everybody has a chance for," she said. Her guest looked puzzled at first, his eyes not sure what to look at or even what to think, until she reached behind him for his wallet.

"Careful there. I am an officer of the law you know and. . . ."

"I'm not taking anything; I'm prepared to give this paltry little wallet something extra, but only if you want it," she said. "But that's for later, right now I am anxious to see Forest Meadow. I want to get my life back, get back on track. If that's where I was at, then take me there."

"That blow on her head came from something—or somebody, maybe Ramona," Caleb told the sheriff the next morning.

"Maybe, but she walked for at least five miles after she left Forest Meadow. She could have fallen down and got the gash on her head that way."

"I suppose."

"You suppose differently?" the sheriff asked.

"Maybe."

"Let me hear it then," the sheriff retorted.

"Maybe Ramona and Stacy had a scuffle when the sinking stopped."

"Or when the house came to rest?" the sheriff offered.

"Maybe. At the least it had to be a time when all movement had stopped, I mean in the yard and the house," Caleb said.

"You mean they had time to be bothered with a petty scuffle between themselves during the time the ground is giving way beneath them? That's hardly likely and furthermore, a scuffle between them over what?" the sheriff asked.

"Like I said sheriff, they scuffled, if they did, not during all the quaking, but when it finished. Furthermore, maybe was that scuffled over was not so petty."

"I'm listening," the sheriff challenged, though at that moment the coroner rang up the sheriff with his autopsy report on the three bodies. The conversation lasted all of sixty seconds and the sheriff put the phone down quietly and turned to Caleb. "Just as I thought. Lady Jasmine died by asphyxiation. Lady Christine died by asphyxiation. Lady Ramona died from collapsed lungs and a punctured heart brought about by a heavy object crushing her upper torso. The coroner thinks that object was none other than the house. Therefore we can rule out any murder and probably even a confrontation at all between Stacy and Ramona. Ramona died one way and Stacy somehow escaped another way. Our hope for anymore reconstruction of what happened out there is lodged in Stacy's memory; the other witnesses are no more. What MacGregor saw and did is hidden in her head right now, but I think a trip to Forest Meadow might help." The sheriff sat back in his chair and folded his hands, before he stood up. "Let's get her out there as soon as we can. You can start by talking to her doctors, maybe this evening if they're around. If not, call them on the phone at home. If they will release her for just a couple hours as soon as tomorrow, plan to bring her out at ten, if that's not too soon for her. And if one of the doctors wants to come along in the morning, no problem, in fact I think I would advise him to do so. I'll want to see you in the morning here before you pick her up, I mean if everything is in order beforehand," the sheriff said.

"Certainly," Caleb replied. His response was all too assured, and he had failed to heed the earlier and prudent warning of the sheriff. Caleb was not such a fool, however, that he could not see Stacy's offer of money for what it was from the previous evening. She was clearly in love with him and was prepared to share her ten years of wages with him and whatever more might be forthcoming as result of Lady Jasmine's death.

"Since you were out here, I thought we might have dinner together, again I mean, if you have time," Stacy said.

"Thank you for the invitation," said Caleb, but maybe let me ring up the sheriff to make sure."

"That's not really necessary is it? I've notice that he doesn't let you make many decisions for yourself."

"Very well, then. If I may ask, has anyone taken you to purchase some clothes and necessities since you've been here?"

"Yes, they did that, but without me, yesterday. I wrote out a little list for them. I wasn't up to it myself. But I do have a shirt and slacks for tomorrow, I mean for going out to see this Forest Meadow."

"What about jewelry?"

"What about jewelry?" Stacy asked.

"Do you wear it?"

"I don't know. Why do you ask," she said.

"Well, your ears are pierced, so you must," Caleb said.

"I suppose so then," she said.

"Could I examine your ear lobes?" he asked.

"Certainly," she said and she turned her head to each side for him. The smell of her perfume made him forget for a brief moment about the coming meal.

"Looks to me like nothing has gone through the piercings lately," he said, before he noticed the jewelry around her neck.

"Where did you get that?" He pointed to a crucifix.

"I don't know."

"But you're wearing it."

"Then it was on me when they found me."

"It's just like another one I've seen," he said, "recently," he added. "I remember now. We found one just like it in Lady Jasmin's possession."

"Lot of good it did her," she said.

"Listen, Stacy, the staff here did give me and the sheriff permission to take you to Forest Meadow tomorrow morning, but they insist that such permission is granted only if you are up to the trip."

"You said that is where I lived, I mean where I came from before the crash."

"Yes, and for ten years."

"I guess so. I do want my memory back, so I'll go."

"You understand you do not have to?"

"Yes, I understand. I know I don't have to go. But I want to go."

"Have you been outside this place since you came? You said you didn't go on the shopping trip yesterday."

"No, haven't been anywhere, but not that I wanted to go anywhere. Until now."

"Listen, how about this: let me ask the staff if I could take you out for dinner right now. That might be good for you in light of the trip in the morning. They haven't brought dinner yet, so let me ask them first. But I do not want to presume—I mean would you want to have dinner out?"

Stacy's face turned a little pale, though she did smile and nodded.

Dinner was uneventful, though her conversation provided pleasant company to Caleb. He did notice that she not infrequently put her utensils down to talk, as if the meal were one thing, and their conversation another thing.

"Caleb, I must tell you that since this morning some of my memory has started to return."

Caleb brought his hand over to hers. "We don't have to go out to Forest Meadow tomorrow," he said.

"No, no. I want to go, still, but you may need to be right with me and maybe we can talk a little in the morning before we get to the place. I mean to settle things, maybe me, down a bit I mean."

"Certainly."

"I know what happened there, I mean everyone has talked about it, pretending they could talk around me, but I heard most everything. I even heard about how you told the sheriff I was nothing special when you and I had a few dates—"

"Stacy, I did not say that! I simply told him I did not know you very well. That is all. I'm sorry if that hearsay hurt you. I could never say that about you, and I'm sorry you heard that. Believe me, I am sorry," Caleb said.

"Well, thank you, that's what I figured. I couldn't see that coming out of you, so it's forgotten, no matter. Anyway I heard a lot about the devastation out there and how awful it looks, but the actual event, I mean when I was there and when it was happening, that's mostly foggy still," she said.

"Stacy, I can't let that go, I mean what you heard. That's awful. Anyway, even if I didn't say it, which I did not, I still feel responsible for the rumor, and I am very sorry," he said.

Stacy smiled and nodded.

"I do remember Forest Meadow as a little bit of paradise, and granted, paradise sunk in the past, but it was lovely to most everyone who was there. I may have trouble with seeing the state of the main house tomorrow, I mean with the beating it took falling into the sinkhole, or so I heard. The staff here has kept newspapers away from me, as best they could I mean, so I still only know mostly what I picked up from you and the sheriff and others. Stacy began a quiet weeping and Caleb motioned to the waitress for his bill, though they had hardly started eating. When they got back to Stacy's room, Caleb placed an arm around her and she lay her head on his shoulder.

"I really did enjoy dinner. Sorry about the tears," she said. Caleb reached over and kissed her softly on the cheek, just before she reached underneath the bed.

"Thank you for your apology tonight, that tells me I can trust you," she added. Stacy moved away from Caleb a little then, but in a couple seconds put both arms around him and kissed him passionately, before she got up and locked her door. "My own finagled key," she said, smiling. I want something more than anything we had in the past," she said and smiled. "But I know everyone suspects me, I mean since I'm the only survivor and three people are dead. I was thinking that we can help each other tomorrow. When I go out to Forest Meadow tomorrow they'll be looking to pin something on me, so I've had to think ahead. You remember when that nice policewoman took me in another room here and found what you told her was on my left thigh? I was thinking that since I'm sure they'll search me tomorrow, you better take all my savings from my ten years work, because I'm sure they'll search me. And if they found it on me, they would claim it as something else."

"Stacy, what are you asking me to do?"

"To put in safekeeping my earnings from ten years of work, until we can enjoy the money together, after tomorrow. Sleep on it tonight and you can take the monies with you when you leave in a little while. I absolutely trust you Caleb, even more than you trust me. But I do love you and I want us to be happy. Happy as never before. And we will be because that trip to Forest Meadow in the morning will clear everything up. I managed to scan my files here a couple hours ago when a stupid nurse left them lying about. They're planning on releasing me tomorrow afternoon. Things could not be looking more up," she said.

Caleb smiled and nodded.

"Meanwhile, we have about thirty minutes before visiting hours are over. Let's make the most of it," she said.

The morning was bright and sunny. The hour Caleb and Stacy began their trek was as hopeful as any late September day could be and at Forest Meadow the day could not have been more beautiful. Stacy began to talk as soon as they were out of the facility parking lot. On the advice of the sheriff earlier that morning, Caleb had brought along a little pocket recorder that he sat up on the dash after showing it to her, and after they had had a brief conversation about the order of the morning events. She kissed him on the cheek after they were out of the sight of people and any traffic. After that Stacy did not look anywhere except straight ahead, while she voiced empty words for the recorder. Caleb refrained from even glancing at her, for fear his gaze would upset her concentration and greater fear that her gaze might prod him to turn the car around.

"Something hit me, maybe a gusset or rafter from the shed. I had thought when I fled from the sinkhole that if I stayed under the protection of that shed I might be safe, but in less than even a minute I started to hear wood members above cracking and then I saw whole timbers coming down, I mean walls and roof. Before I could run out from underneath, something fell in front of me and something above hit me from behind. I guess that's where my head gash came from. After that I don't remember anything, not even the person who picked me up on the road."

Caleb pulled over. "We're only about a couple miles away."

"Okay, I need to compose myself a little more. Try that driveway up there for now. I need to think for a moment."

An older man soon came ambling down the driveway and now headed toward his visitors.

"Who is that?" Caleb asked.

"Looks like a neighbor. A neighbor we hardly ever saw and had very little contact with. Forest Meadow was never known for much neighborliness."

"Looks like he wants to talk," Caleb said, when the man was within earshot of the car.

"You're Stacy?" he said, now coming to Stacy's side of the car.

"Yes. I am. You must be Mr. Boulder?"

"That would be me," he said. "Really sorry to hear about what happened over there. I don't know how you made it out when nobody else did."

Caleb motioned to Stacy.

She nodded.

"If I can be of any help later on, do let me know. I am close by, always have been," he said and Stacy presented a weak smile back to him."

"Thank you Mr. Boulder," she said, as Caleb backed the car down the driveway. Mr. Boulder waved.

"Don't suppose he saw or heard anything that day?" Caleb asked when they were far enough away.

"No. Too far away."

"Maybe he saw you staggering about afterward?"

"Doubtful. He's no worry. We can go to Forest Meadow now," she said, and she motioned toward the recorder still on the dash. He reached up and switched it off.

"Are you ready?" he asked.

She nodded.

The sheriff's car and a car with a doctor from the institution sat parked on the roadside. Caleb drove onto the wrecked property, and found some flat ground off the side of the driveway and right next to the damaged house.

"Lady MacGregor, thank you for coming out here this morning. The hospital staff told me they may release you this afternoon," the sheriff said.

"So I've heard," she said, smiling, before she turned around and walked about three steps before she lost her breakfast in a half dozen heaves. Caleb walked over and insisted on wiping her mouth with his handkerchief.

She finally stood up, while the men remained silent.

"Well, where shall I start?" and she wiped her mouth again before tears came again.

"Lady MacGregor, are you sure you're up to this because we can do it another day if need be?" the sheriff asked.

"I am," she said, but she started to quiver a bit and her speech suffered interruption with halting words. The beautiful though chilly autumn morning sent Caleb back to his patrol car for Stacy's jacket. In another minute he had placed it over her shoulders, though the jacket zipped up tightly against a bosom that the psychologist and the sheriff noticed.

"I suppose you want to hear everything. My memory has almost returned entirely, in fact, my memory of my prior dating relationship with your detective Caleb came back just this morning, as he drove me over here. In felt good not to be in the company of any stranger anymore. And detective I did not mean to startle you in the car when suddenly memory of you returned. But anyway, recovered memory doesn't make it any easier for me to see all of this. I truly adored this place."

"So, if you would Lady MacGregor, tells us what happened that afternoon," the sheriff politely asked.

"Certainly. After two of us were buried in dirt, and with only Ramona and me left, and knowing we could do nothing for either of the dead, we scrambled around the yard for a while, and I'm sure we must have been screeching all the time, as more ground collapsed downward and fell into the expanding sinkhole and our fright only became worse."

"Excuse me, Lady Macgregor. You saw the both of them, Jasmin and Christine, go down?" asked the sheriff.

"Yes. We all were outside for not more than a half minute, and just a few steps clear of the house, when suddenly I hear this ferocious sound, something like a herd of wild elephants stampeding or the sound of lions roaring at the top of their lungs. That very moment, the ground in front of Lady Scott collapsed while her walker went first and then her body fell into plummeting earth. Odd as it seems I don't recall even a scream from her. I figured later that maybe her mouth and head were buried so quickly and that's why we heard nothing, not even a muffled or muted scream. And then another huge chunk of ground collapses straight downward again and Christine falls out of sight."

"And that was the last you saw of either of them?"

"Yes."

"So what did you do then?' the sheriff continued.

"It seemed everywhere we sought for safety the ground started sinking. We jumped around, hoping for something that might be stable enough for sure footing in a sea of moving earth. The thought raced through my brain that this was maybe the end of the world, and I remember grabbing the crucifix around my neck in one hand. Our next thought was to try to go back into the house, but at the same time we see one side of the house lurch upward and then hear the structure starting to crack in places and starting to tip on one side. In a matter of a couple minutes, the gorgeous and stately main house, just repainted this summer, has slipped off the foundation and pulled away from the sides and was soon tottering on the edge of the sinkhole."

"Take a breath," Caleb said to Stacy and she turned away for a second before resuming her story.

"Ramona and I decided we might have a chance with the big oak in the side yard, but had no idea if this was a viable plan because the upturned house blocked any view of the tree, so we weren't sure it was even still upright. In another minute we saw the tree, and we made it to the base, but neither one of us was meant for climbing trees, I mean at forty years of age and not in the best shape, so we decided we needed a ladder. I was just about to go to the shed to get one, even though we really didn't know if there were ladders there, but Ramona reached out and stopped me, because in what seemed like an instant most all of the shaking of the ground stopped. The only thing we heard then was an occasional growling of the ground that we presumed was resettling noise. We began to think maybe the trauma of heaving ground was about over and maybe over for good.

Suddenly Ramona begins to tell me that the bonuses we were scheduled to get on the death of Lady Scott might get tied up in court with her death because of the circumstance and that maybe we ought to go in the house, careful like, and get our money before it got tied up in some court where it might not be ours for some time."

"Lady MacGregor, didn't you think that an odd thing to be bringing up in your circumstances at the time?" the sheriff asked.

"Most certainly I did and I told her. More than that I thought it really disrespectful toward the two people who had just perished, I mean that Ramona could think of Lady Jasmin's money with her having died only minutes before."

"So, you did tell her that?" the sheriff continued.

"Of course and I hollered it at her, at least twice. I was against the whole idea of someone's death being to my gain. There was also the fact that going into the house would be dangerous, but Ramona was almost always indifferent to fear and she was persuasive, even as I mustered courage enough to disagree with her. With the danger of more sinking earth, she nevertheless continued her argument about getting the money inside outside as fast as we could. Though I continued to offer some objections, she didn't want to hear my objections anymore, she said. We had to do, not debate, she said. Finally, and against all my warnings, she went into the house alone and got her bonus money and mine and left the rest—or so she said, and with what she showed me, I think that was true. But I don't know how she knew where that money was kept—because Lady Scott didn't trust any bank and hid it somewhere no one except Jasmine knew about, not even us, but apparently Ramona did. She was the sneaky type and Lady Jasmine, God rest her soul, never really figured that out about her."

"But you did?"

"Yes. You don't live with someone for ten years without getting to know them."

"But apparently Lady Jasmine didn't figure that out about her, I mean over the same ten years?" the sheriff asked.

"I guess not," Stacy responded, looking a bit miffed at the sheriff because of his question.

"So you got nowhere with Ramona, I mean about the money and going into the tottering house for it?" the sheriff inquired.

"Nowhere at all. She was adamant to get in the house and get that money," Lady MacGregor said.

"Go on."

"Well, the house looked like it swayed just a little when Ramona went into it, but I'm not sure. I kept shouting from outside that she needed to get out, fearing the whole thing might topple down into the sinkhole and take her down with it. She told me when she got back outside and was out of breath, that she was not in there more than about three minutes and she knew that because that's how long she could hold her breath and did. More importantly, I figured that within that time she must have gone directly to the money and that meant for sure that she knew exactly where big stashes were kept. I myself, nor Christine, had any idea where Lady Scott kept her stash."

"But after she came out of the house, what did the two of you do then?" the sheriff asked. "And what happened to the money she got from inside? We found no money on Ramona or in any of the dirt here," the sheriff added.

"Well, as soon as she was back out she told me to give her my key to that door. For some reason hers was still inside and she thought it in her bureau in her room she said, but it was too dangerous to go back inside she insisted, and I couldn't but agree at the moment. She said she needed to lock the door in case trespassers and vandals tried to break in and steal stuff and they would for certain be thieves once people heard what had happened at Forest Meadow. That made sense because everyone thought of this place as steeped in all kinds of old things, with valuable jewels and the like just lying about. Because her warning made perfect sense to me, I went along and gave her the key."

"Did she give it back to you?" the sheriff asked.

Caleb looked at Stacy, but only for a second.

"Not at first, but when I made a huge fuss, she did."

"And that was the key in your pocket, I mean when you were found on the road and they brought you to the hospital?"

"Yes. I was adamant to end up with the key because I was starting to suspect that Ramona planned to go back in the house again when it was safe enough, I mean to get the rest of the money and heaven knows what else."

"But, Lady MacGregor, you forced her to give the key back to you. How would she have gotten back in? " the sheriff asked.

"Easy. She would have squeezed in the house, without going through a door, like she did the first time, and that with not too much trouble. But none of that matters, because she never made it back into the house."

"How do you know that?" the sheriff asked, already suspicious that something was not adding up with this story.

"Well, the first thing she did, I mean after she came out of the upturned house gasping almost like she had nearly drowned, she showed me a wad of money, her $100,000 she said, and she very quickly counted it out in front of me before she put it in the pocket of her slacks. She claimed there had been three bundles of equal amount inside, one for each lady, but vowed that she had not touched what would have been Christine's portion. After Ramona put that first wad of money into her right side slacks pocket, then she pulled out another. It was just like the first one in amount or so she said, though she didn't count that one out and instead just handed it to me. I didn't really know what I should do. When I told her I could not take it and would not, she pretended to be upset with me, but put it in the pocket of her slacks, like the other money, and claimed she would keep it for me until things settled down."

"So, you ending up with none of that money and her with all of it?"

"Yes. I'm not a penny richer for what happened her."

"Any you haven't seen any of that money since?" the sheriff asked.

"None of it," Stacy answered.

"And so she, I mean Ramona, carried it all, presumably $200,000?" the sheriff asked.

"Yes. For a few seconds I considered trying to wrestle both wads of money from her or out of her and return them to the house, but I soon saw this was impossible."

Lady MacGregor's words stopped suddenly and a torrent of tears began to issue from her. "I suppose if I had been strong enough, I mean mentally and physically, I could have overpowered her to get the money, but suddenly the ground starting shifting and gyrating every which away again, so I headed for the shed and for a ladder, resuming our original plan of scaling up the tree."

"And how about Ramona?" the sheriff asked.

"I'm not precisely sure, but I do know that as I ran toward the shed I shouted back to her that I would be back quickly, but as soon as I got underneath the roof of the shed, I heard the cracking of the house again and a loud tumbling noise, like a huge garbage can being rolled over. I felt a sinking feeling in my stomach then that the house was collapsing into the sinkhole and I turned just in time to see the dust thrown up and the house tumbling down into the giant hole. Just a little while later, maybe only five seconds or so, I heard a terrifying scream and I grabbed my crucifix from around my neck and prayed that Ramona was okay. I figured she had gone back into the house and was crushed inside it when the structure fell into the hole, but I'm not sure."

"But you didn't go to look for her or to help?" the sheriff asked.

"No, and I couldn't, because just about exactly at that same time I got hit on the head in the collapsing shed, which knocked me unconscious. You know the rest of my story from there," she said.

"Well, we found no money, much less any of $200,000 in Ramona's clothing. And we found no money in the personal effects of Lady Jasmine or Lady Christine. So unless you have it, Lady MacGregor, it must still be down in that dirt somewhere—and we've already been through it twice with a fine toothed comb. Do you have any notion where it might be, because I am inclined to think you must have the missing money? And by the way, was your account of the money tussle between you and Ramona something that you just recalled this morning? You related no such episode to any of us before. In fact, if Lady Jasmine's accountant and my officers had not done some preliminary searches for money in the house and compared that with her accountant, we would not even be raising the question of missing monies, nor would you needed even have told us about the money."

"So, if I had wanted to be untruthful, I could have kept the money to myself and told no one, but I didn't did I? That should tell you I am being honest and forthright with you!"

"Well, Lady MacGregor, it should, but it doesn't. Because there is still the matter of $200,000 to account for, that you admit to seeing. But there is something more. The accountant and we together found close to $300,000 unaccounted for. She always kept that secluded in the house, so the accountant told us. Apparently that amount was intended for each of you three ladies. So your untold story is that you, not Ramona, went in the house by yourself for the last $100,000, but before that you somehow got the $200,000 from Ramona, for a total of $300,000. I don't know how you did that but you did. If you have anything that can controvert the trail of the missing money, I am prepared to listen, but before you speak again, I suggest you enlist a lawyer," the sheriff said.

Caleb had a sudden sinking feeling that he had unwisely plotted with a thief who was as prepared to cheat him as she was Christine and Ramona.

"Do you know where that money is, for if you do, that would come close to tying this whole mess up?" the sheriff asked, looking on at Stacy.

"I'm afraid I do, but it will give me a little pain to tell you," Stacy said.

"More painful than a few years of prison time?" the sheriff said.

Caleb leaned over and proceeded to throw his breakfast up onto the ground. Stacy watched as he grabbed the handkerchief that he had used for her out of his pocket, while managing to right himself enough to request a private conversation with the sheriff. The sheriff was too close to making his final case to be deviated from the immediate task by anyone, even his deputy.

Before going out to Forest Meadow that morning, the sheriff had requested a female officer come out about 10:30 and now she drove up. Everyone knew in what direction the investigation was pointing, for the police, Caleb included, had known for thirty six hours about the missing money. Though most everything pointed to Lady MacGregor as a prime suspect, Caleb was naïve enough to consider Stacy's account from the prior evening over the evidence of his boss, capped off by a tempting taste of what life might be like with a woman with whom he had previously been non-committal. Meanwhile Lady MacGregor, ahead of both Caleb and the sheriff, would not be totally bested by any maneuver of law enforcement and had padded her bra that morning.

Caleb had laid himself open with more vulnerabilities than he could manage in the presence of a subtle and vengeful woman. After she had teased and seduced him, he was in effect hers and she went ahead with her devious plan as she gambled that Caleb would not rat her out. How well her trap worked depended on how well she had assessed Caleb for opportunity to have her revenge and the morning confirmed that all was well for her, beyond a little prison time. Caleb would be an accomplice in her crime of theft, and that trap laid as result of resentment of a prior dating relationship that had scarcely attracted him to her and she knew it.

Knowing law enforcement suspected she would have the money hidden, Stacy would have her final bit of fun with the police. The female officer took Stacy inside the once majestic house at Forest Meadow, the damaged house now returned to an at least upright position on a reasonably flat surface. The female officer took her inside and proceeded to search her from head to toe, though she found no wadded money. The men outside stood waiting and in another few minutes the female officer walked out with Stacy beside her. Stacy's head was erect and her face looking pleased as she stepped on the ground that had once been the unwrinkled lawn of the stately mansion of Forest Meadow. The officer shook her head at the sheriff and the sheriff pointed for her to take Lady McGregor to the sheriff's car. Caleb, with hesitation, made a couple steps toward Stacy as she was put in the back of the vehicle.

"You're going to charge me as a suspect, though you found no such money in my possession," MacGregor said to the sheriff.

"Oh, we'll find the money. It only got away from us temporarily."

"I could help with that," she said.

"Is that so?" the sheriff said.

Caleb jumped to the sheriff's side asking again for a private conference, and again being repulsed.

"I had a little help hiding it, I mean helping a hopeful someone hide it. If I help a little with your search, could you help me a little with lightening my sentence?"

"That could be arranged. What have you got?"

"Oh, I don't have anything. He has everything."

"Not sure I understand," the sheriff said.

"Neither will he," she said, pointing to Caleb.

"You can't be serious?" The sheriff look stunned.

"I'd put my whole rotten life on it," she said. "I heard word of what he said about me, and strangely enough, some of it tumbled from you in an idle moment. Got to watch what you say sheriff, it may come around to bite you or those around you. By the way, make sure all $300, 000 is there because that's what he took from me. Meanwhile, I'll have more satisfaction from his imprisonment than I ever would have had with that money—or him," she laughed.

The sheriff turned aside from the car and then leaned over and proceeded to throw up onto the ground. His deputy Paul grabbed a handkerchief for the sheriff who remained bent over.